Endorsements

Jeanne Nigro has gone beneath the surface of the end times to teach us how and why we should not live in a spirit of fear during these tempestuous days. She helps us understand that the events of this world are not falling apart...they are falling into place. As God's children we need not fall apart either. Jeanne Nigro will bless you through her incredible knowledge of the end times.

Dr. H. Dean Haun
Senior Pastor
First Baptist Church
Morristown, TN

As the world around us spirals out of control and many are overwhelmed with fear and uncertainty, *Unshaken* provides a solution...draw near to God! Jeanne offers great strategies for breaking out of our busy schedules and intensely fast-paced lives to find intimacy with God again – the only true antidote to fear.

Jonathan Bernis
President and CEO
Jewish Voice Ministries, International

Jeanne Nigro, like myself, has been a passionate advocate for the Kingdom of God through teaching, speaking and practical life experience. In her latest offering entitled *Unshaken*, she attacks straight on the greatest adversaries of our daily peace and confidence with solid Biblical truth and hard hitting life experiences. But she doesn't leave you by simply recognizing the problem, she finishes with ten solid action points to implement the antidote for the systemic problems of our culture. Her insights for the celebration of the Feasts of the Lord will also encourage you to live a

Kingdom lifestyle with joy and freedom! Mature and passionate are the two words that come to mind; enjoy!

PAUL WILBUR
Integrity Music Artist

The world is in the most unstable, chaotic, insecure, and shakable position it has ever been in. Everything we have previously thought was a sure foundation, from the economy to the very fibers of morality, is being shaken. However, Jeanne has done an outstanding job of bringing a fresh new perspective of hope for a future rooted and grounded in the love and goodness of God. She is precise in pointing out that our relationship with God is the one thing that cannot be shaken nor taken from the true believer. Her practical steps for developing a closer, more personal relationship with the Lord will prove to be invaluable to every believer. Truly this is a book written for such a time as this and for a future that is sure and unshakeable with the Lord at the center of our lives.

PASTOR SANDRA G. KENNEDY
Founder and Senior Pastor
Whole Life Ministries

I am happy to endorse *Unshaken* because of the enormous amount of fear that is coming at families from many different sources. Fear can operate much like the prophetic except in the opposite direction. Fear is assuming something of the unseen that has not manifested yet but its affects drive us to anxiety and confusion.

Jeanne Nigro has locked in on some principles that will help guide us in the future to not be driven with fear of the future. She will stir hope alive within you so you are not overtaken by unexpected events. She weaves personal experiences with Biblical truths to enforce your faith and build a foundation that will withstand the onslaught of days to come.

I think you will learn while being inspired to move forward and break out of the paralysis of fear.

KERRY KIRKWOOD
Pastor of Trinity Fellowship in Tyler, Texas

As so many believers are becoming increasingly paralyzed by fear and passivity, what we need right now is a heaven sent word of encouragement. Jeanne Nigro has provided us with just that—a true well of solid teaching and genuine wisdom for our time.

JOEL RICHARDSON
New York Times bestselling author of
Islamic Antichrist and *Mideast Beast*
International expert and speaker on
biblical prophecy, the Middle East, and Islam.

Every person should be concerned for the future. Why is that? Because every person is going to spend the rest of their lives in the future. Less the result of circumstances, the quality of our future will, in so many ways, be ultimately determined by how we think and how we act today! While many are soul sick and shaken by sin and circumstance, my friend Jeanne Nigro offers some remedial biblical medicine for life's assorted hurts—stuff to enable us to be unshaken. I'm pleased to recommend her upbeat, biblically based work.

DR. JEFFREY L. SEIF
Professor, Kings University

In an hour filled with confusion, deception and every wind of doctrine, it is encouraging to know that the LORD is raising up dedicated teachers of the Word of God, who have understanding of the times and speak clearly into the state and future destiny of His Church. In *Unshaken*, Jeanne Nigro answers the philosophical and practical questions of the hour with unparalleled revelation and clarity, making the practical day-to-day application both simple and extremely relevant to your spiritual growth. Therefore, it is my great joy and privilege to recommend *Unshaken*. May it be a guiding light that strengthens your intimacy with Jesus and causes you to stand victorious before Him at His coming!

COREY STARK
Senior Leader IHOPKC Missions Base.

Unshaken

STANDING STRONG
in Uncertain Times

Jeanne Nigro

DESTINY IMAGE® PUBLISHERS, INC.
P.O. Box 310, Shippensburg, PA 17257-0310
"Promoting Inspired Lives."

This book and all other Destiny Image and Destiny Image Fiction books are available at Christian bookstores and distributors worldwide.

Cover design by Eileen Rockwell

For more information on foreign distributors, call 717-532-3040.
Reach us on the Internet: www.destinyimage.com.

ISBN 13 TP: 978-0-7684-0999-4
ISBN 13 eBook: 978-0-7684-1012-9

For Worldwide Distribution, Printed in the U.S.A.
2 3 4 5 6 7 8 / 20 19 18 17 16

Dedication

I dedicate this book to the beautiful family that God has so graciously given me—my husband Al and daughter Charis. Without their unending love, support, prayers, understanding, patience, and forgiveness—there would be no *Unshaken*. I would also like to honor Nancy Missler, my first spiritual mentor, who went to be with Jesus while I was writing this book. I began working with her ministry just months after I became a believer 27 years ago, and her life and teachings significantly shaped the foundations of my relationship with the Lord and my ministry.

Acknowledgments

I would like to acknowledge the following ministries—Koinonia House, Healing for the Nations, International House of Prayer, and Wellspring Ministries—whose concepts have in some shape or form been woven into the content of this book. They have become an integral part of my own ministry teachings due to the significant impact they have had on my life. I also want to thank my friend Rich Nicholson. If he had not been so faithful, persistent, and loving in sharing (and debating!) about God when I was so broken and lost 28 years ago that I wanted to end my life, I would not be alive today to share God's message. Rich, I am eternally grateful; may you be abundantly rewarded in the Millennium!

Contents

Introduction

On a lifelong search for truth, fulfillment, and the meaning of life, at 24 I moved by myself from Ohio to Southern California after graduate school. Growing up "emotionally disconnected," I found that music (what's now referred to as "classic rock") and concerts enabled me to feel, so I set out to pursue the music business in Los Angeles. Quickly disheartened by the business side of music, I then proceeded to try out as many different jobs and careers as possible—marketing research, advertising, neuropsychology, waitressing, staffing nurses, corporate training, management consulting, quality improvement, organizational psychology—you name it and I probably tried it! I was desperate to find something that I believed in, that "my heart was into." If someone would have told me 30 years ago that I'd find what I was searching for in God and that I'd end up having a teaching ministry and writing this book, I would have told them they were nuts! There was no way I could ever believe in the God of the Bible; I was way too enlightened for that! It just goes to show, if you're truly, truly searching for truth, you'll eventually find it in God.

Well, one of the many careers that I pursued during that time of searching was consumer research for advertising agencies.

Somehow, I would always end up on automotive accounts. Not exactly the perfect job fit for me! Before a new advertisement for a car or truck was released on a national level, we would conduct focus groups in selected key markets. Often I would travel to Dallas to test truck ads—never imagining that one day I would live there and have a daughter whose "dream car" is a Silverado truck!

When I set out to write this book, *Unshaken: Standing Strong in Uncertain Times*, I had no idea that *I* would be the test market, and that as I was writing I would have to apply each word to my own life. For example, when I state that intimacy with God is the only thing that we need and that can't be taken away from us, can *I* really stand strong on that when everything in my life is so uncertain in this season?

I share this only because I want you to know as you begin this book that every page you read was written out of my own life experience. I have struggled with fear, discouragement, and doubt due to uncertainties in my own life and in the world, yet as I applied each principle in this book, it has withstood the test.

On those days when I held on with all my might to the anchors for the soul that you will discover in this book, no matter what my circumstances were telling me, I experienced His presence. It is in His presence that we have fullness of joy, which is our strength.

> *In Your presence is fullness of joy; at Your right hand are pleasures forevermore* (Psalms 16:11).

> *The joy of the Lord is your strength* (Nehemiah 8:10).

However, on days when I let go of these anchors, I nearly drowned in a sea of self-pity, fear, stress, doubt, negativity, abandonment, frustration, and anger. Now how's that for a description of a victim!

Focusing on these anchors enabled me to stand strong, gave me joy and hope in the midst of uncertainty, and placed me not just *above* water, but walking *on* the water with Jesus. You see, my goal in writing this book is not just that you would survive uncertain times, but that you would *thrive* with Him in uncertain times!

My heart's desire is that you experience the abundant life only Jesus can bring in the midst of your circumstances. When the rest of the world is consumed in fear of the end times, I want them to see something different in you. I want your life to be a light and a testimony to all around you of the faithfulness, love, and power of God, regardless of how dark our world becomes. We all yearn for revival, but first *we* must be lights so that the world desires to be revived! Lastly, I want you to experience the fulfillment of purpose, joy, and healing that comes from connecting with the many facets of God's heart and partnering with His passions for these times.

These are exciting times to be alive, and it's no mistake that you are here on this earth right now! Don't go wishing that you were still back in the '60s or '70s or even 10 years ago. You have been appointed for such a time as this! Consider it a privilege and an honor to be alive and be used by God to release His power and accomplish His purposes in these end times! Don't dread, commiserate with others, or hide out, but take hold of these anchors that God has given you to stand strong and unshaken and you will experience His abundant life in the midst of the uncertainties in your own life and in the world around you.

You, like I did, will have a choice to make as you read each page of this book. That is a Deuteronomy 30:19 choice between life and death; between sinking or walking on the water, between fear, stress, frustration, anger, and negativity or Jesus' abundant life. I pray that you will choose life and that you will hold tight to the anchors revealed in this book. I'm excited to explore them with you, but first I'd like to share my own "Paralyzed by Fear," experience that was the catalyst for writing *Unshaken: Standing Strong in Uncertain Times.*

> *I call heaven and earth as witnesses today against you, that I have set before you life and death, blessing and cursing; therefore choose life, that both you and your descendants may live* (Deuteronomy 30:19).

Chapter 1

Paralyzed by Fear

My daughter often asks me for help late at night with her English homework, and one night she asked me for an example of "situational irony." Well here's a perfect example!

After a long day of teaching on "experiencing freedom from fear," there I was, that same evening, completely consumed in fear! *Paralyzed* is the best way to describe it, so fearful that I couldn't think, move, or feel! Why? I was fearing these uncertain end times, and I don't think I'm the only one who has ever felt that way!

The End Times Epidemic

Fear and stress from the times in which we live seem to be overtaking many of us, regardless of our faith. All you have to do is watch the news or scroll through social media pages for five minutes and you're injected with a dose of fear and stress about the economy, terrorism, ISIS, rampant immorality, racial riots, religious persecution, gun control, threat of world wars, nuclear attacks, coming judgment, U.S. decline as a global power, rise of Islam and Sharia law, instability in the Middle East, Muslim refugees…and the list goes on. Add to that the uncertainty in our personal lives from our jobs, relationships, finances, and health and we've got a culture who's generally fearful, stressed, angry, or frustrated and is either lashing out or hiding under the covers—neither of which is God's plan and desire for us.

On the contrary, they are the enemy's plan for us. Satan is working through our fear and busyness to keep us stressed out, distracted, checked out, feeling powerless, and believing there is nothing we can do except wait for Jesus' return. He wants us so focused and consumed with our own problems and crazy schedules that we don't have the energy to care about the bigger picture and open our eyes to the deception overtaking us (both from outside and inside the church). We look just like everyone else and we are ineffective in what God is calling us to do in these times!

Jesus warned us in Luke 21:25–36 that our hearts would fail from fear in the last days if we focused our eyes on the distress of the nations (or the news!). However, if we *watched*—if we paid attention to the signs of the times and studied what is on God's heart for the end times as revealed in His Word; and *prayed* --which aligns us with God's heart, releases His power in our situations, and deepens our intimacy with Him --we would be able to stand strong in victory in the midst of these uncertain end times.

> *And there will be signs in the sun, in the moon, and in the stars; and on the earth distress of nations, with perplexity, the sea and the waves roaring; men's hearts failing them from fear and the expectation of those things which are coming on the earth, for the powers of the heavens will be shaken…. But take heed to yourselves, lest your hearts be weighed down with carousing, drunkenness, and cares of this life, and that Day come on you unexpectedly. For it will come as a snare on all those who dwell on the face*

of the whole earth. Watch therefore, and pray always that you may have strength to escape all these things that will come to pass, and to stand before the Son of Man (Luke 21:25-26,34-36).

Well before I get ahead of myself and jump too far ahead, let's get back to the story.

Disoriented and Hopeless

As I mentioned before, I had just finished teaching a seminar on "experiencing freedom from fear," yet there I was at midnight the same night, wandering aimlessly through the hotel parking lot, disoriented and bewildered, feeling hopeless and completely paralyzed by fear. Now I knew in my head all the reasons why I shouldn't fear—after all I had just taught them that same day! No, my fear wasn't from lack of "head knowledge." Somehow, everything I taught seemed to be lost in outer space, suddenly unreachable, untouchable, unable to break through the paralysis of fear I was experiencing. Fear, that is, of being overtaken by terrorism, financial collapse, religious persecution, beheadings, famine, becoming a military state, and more! You see, I had attended a dinner that evening with people who had "high level intelligence" about what was in store for our country in the coming months. I couldn't wait to get filled in and connected with this secretive "in-the-know" group!

However, they shared nightmare after nightmare about what was going to happen in the next month and coming years, and by the time I returned to my hotel that night I was in a complete state of paralysis. I felt that our future was so hopeless, so set in stone, so horrific that I didn't even want to live another day! What's the point if it's all going to end this way and there's nothing I can do about it? What good would my teaching do? Why should I even send my daughter to school the next day? We should just spend our last days together huddled at home, grasping every last minute that we can together. And I was certain it was all going to end this way; after all, someone with such authority and military intelligence said so!

The Roots of My Fear

Allow me to digress for a few moments (or pages) because this is critical for you to know if you truly want to break free from fear and remain unshaken in these end times. My first mistake that night was to put these people on a pedestal of authority and assume that everything they said was absolute and certain truth. In other words, I took God off the throne and put them on in His place! Now looking back, I realize that my tendency to put others on a pedestal and believe that I have to take in as truth whatever they "throw at me" is rooted in some very old strongholds of mine. We'll cover this in much more detail in Chapter 4 of this book, but basically when I use the word *strongholds* I mean those old messages that we all receive growing up—from our parents, teachers, coaches, authority figures, even our culture and religion. They are lies that we believe about ourselves and they cause us to believe lies about God. In fact, they cause us to put other peoples' faces on Him!

You see, being the youngest of seven, I received messages not only from my mom and dad, but also from four older brothers and two older sisters! That's a lot of messages! In fact, I could fill the rest of this chapter with those messages! Don't worry, I won't hit you with *all* of them right now, but just to give you an idea, here are a few of my favorites: *"I don't have a voice, I don't exist, I have to take whatever comes at me, I'm worthless, I'm bad, I'm not as good/valuable as you, I have nothing to offer, What I have to say isn't important, I'm not worth your time or attention, I can't question anything that I'm told, I have to disappear, I'm unprotected, I'm on my own, I'm all alone, I can't break through your wall."* Can *you* relate to any of these?

Well those messages cause me (and you) to believe all kinds of lies about God, and I think every one of them got activated that night! Did you know that whenever you fear or stress (which is the "socially acceptable" word for fear) you are *always* believing a lie about God? Otherwise you wouldn't fear or stress. So in order to break free of fear and stress, it's critical that you become aware of the lies you're believing both about yourself and about God!

Where Was God in the Picture?

For me that night, I was believing that God had disappeared, abandoned me—that He was no longer with me or protecting me, and that He was basically "non-existent." Because it is the end times, He has no more involvement in my life or with anything "down here" until He returns to this earth. From now until then, He is just going to stand back, watch it all happen, and allow evil to reign. He's completely pulling out of the battle, and I'm left in it alone to fight for myself. To sum it up, He just flat out disappeared and was out of the picture of my life!

What do I mean by *out of the picture*? Whenever you find yourself flooded with fearful, anxious, or negative thoughts, it is important to ask God to show you, "Where are You, God, in the picture?" Now in your head, the answer to that question might seem obvious; after all, Hebrews 13:5 tells you that He will never leave you nor forsake you. However, most of the time, the answer *in your heart* is that "He's not in the picture," that you've taken Him out for various reasons and/or believe He's just watching but unable or unwilling to protect you. After all, if you *really* believed He was in the picture, would you ever fear, stress, dread, or doubt?

We often take God out of the picture if our earthly fathers (or whoever was supposed to be protecting us) just sat back and watched, were distant, didn't protect us, or were absent from the picture of our lives.

Some examples of the lies you might believe about God are:

- He's distant. He is too busy with bigger problems than yours. He's not interested or not with you in every aspect of your life.

- *Your* job is to hold everything and everyone together. He's not dependable—sometimes He's there and sometimes He's not. *You're* the only one you can depend on.

Each of us believe different lies depending on the messages we received growing up, but we are all alike in that we received them when we were young, we took them into our hearts as truth, and they began to determine our thoughts, emotions, words, attitudes, and actions for the rest of our lives!

Regardless of what we know in our heads to be true about who God is, our hearts will believe these old messages unless we allow God to heal our hearts, which thankfully He loves to do!

I'm sharing this now because it will help you to understand what I was experiencing that night in my paralysis of fear. You see, even though I knew the truth (my goodness, I had been teaching the truth all weekend), my heart was believing those old stronghold messages about myself and God, and as a result I allowed the fear, paralysis, hopelessness, abandonment, and disorientation to set in. So let's get back to where I left off in my "Paralyzed by Fear" story.

I finally made my way back to my hotel room, but I could not settle down enough to sleep. I headed to the hotel fitness center and walked as fast as I could on the treadmill shouting out loud (there was no one else in the room at 1 a.m.), "Thank You that You have not given me a spirit of fear," and I tried to *exercise* the physical symptoms of fear out of my body.

The Lies We Believe

Eventually, I was able to sleep that night, and in the morning I decided it was time to practice what I preach. God always desires to reveal truth in the inmost places of our hearts, so I asked Him to show me what lies I was believing about myself and about Him that were causing me to react in such an extreme state of shut down paralysis.

Once again, it is *so* important to ask Him, "Where are You in this picture, God?" or maybe more appropriately, "Where have I put You in this picture, God?" When you ask God to reveal truth, He is *always* faithful to do so. His heart is always to heal your heart! I've listed below all He revealed that I was believing, and as you're reading this list think about whether you've ever felt this way:

Lies About Myself:

- I'm unprotected.
- I'm all alone.
- I have to fight for myself.
- I'm on my own now.
- I'm totally abandoned.
- There's no hope, there's nothing that can be done, there's nothing I can do to make a difference, this outcome is set in stone.

- I can't question messages from authority.

- I have to take in whatever is spoken to me.

- I'm not going to make it.

Lies About God

- He's not with me.

- He abandoned me.

- He disappeared.

- He's non-existent.

- He's out of the picture.

- He's just watching until He comes back.

- He's not getting involved.

- He's pulled out completely and is letting evil reign.

- He doesn't care what happens to me.

- He doesn't care about the details of my life.

- He won't protect me.

- He's not accessible.

- I can't break through His wall.

The Spiritual Battle Behind Fear

When God shows us these lies, the only way we can break free from them is to use spiritual weapons of warfare.

Second Corinthians 10:4 tells us that "the weapons of our warfare are not carnal but mighty in God for pulling down strongholds," and Ephesians 6:12 emphasizes, "For we do not wrestle against flesh and blood, but against principalities, against powers, against the rulers of the darkness of this age, against spiritual hosts of wickedness in the heavenly places."

Therefore, our battle (in this case against fear) is not against flesh and blood—that is what we *can* see. Rather, our true battle is against what we *cannot* see in this world with our earthly eyes.

So if our battle is not of this world and not of the flesh, how do we think using earthly or fleshly weapons (which rely on our own strength and wisdom) will ever free us from fear? They can't and they won't. Have you ever tried to stop fear by trying not to think about it, telling someone else about it, running from it, or by just plain shutting down so you don't have to feel it (or anything else)? Well, I've tried all of these fleshly weapons and I can confidently say that none of them work, not in the long run and not for true freedom!

That's because we have to see that fear is more than just an emotion, although oftentimes a justified one, it's a weapon that our enemy uses against us in the unseen, very real, spiritual battle.

That's right. Fear and stress are more than just emotions, your personality, "just the way you are," or an unavoidable and even expected part of life in this culture. They are tools or weapons the enemy uses against you to take you down. The enemy always comes to *steal, kill, and destroy* (see John 10:10). He desires to take away life, to stop progress, and to cause you to go backward. That's exactly what happens when you take in the fear that the enemy shoots your way with his fiery darts! Fear leads to paralysis, hopelessness; it brings death and disease to your bodies, emotions, relationships, and your ability to fulfill the purposes and blessings that God has for your life.

To break free from fear, it's critical to understand that fear is from the *enemy*, not from God! *"For God has not given us a spirit of fear, but of power and of love and of a sound mind"* (2 Tim. 1:7). Satan gets a handle in your life through fear (I like to use the illustration of a rope keeping me tied in bondage to the enemy) regardless of whether or not the fear is justified. He doesn't say, "Oh the fear is justified, I won't get a handle here, I won't get involved!" He'll take any opening you give him.

Satan desperately wants influence in your life any way he can so that he can block God's purposes for you and bring death to your body, emotions, and relationships with others and with God. He wants you to become so fearful and stressed about what is going on in the world that you feel paralyzed, you look and act just as fearful and stressed out as anyone who doesn't believe in Jesus, and all you want to do is pull the covers over your head and hide out until Jesus returns. The enemy loves it when we respond this way to the end times. He has no authority in your life unless you give it to him, and you give him openings or handles when you fear or stress. Remember when I said that behind the fear is *always* a lie that you believe about yourself and about God? Well, who is the father of lies? Where do lies come from? Lies are *always* from Satan; he is the father of lies. *"When he speaks a lie, he speaks from his own resources, for he is a liar and the father of it"* (John 8:44). When you're believing lies about yourself and God, you're aligning yourself with Satan—with his thoughts and his emotions—and you are increasing his reign over your heart.

Do you want to align yourself with Satan's strategies for you in these end times or with God's? The choice is yours!

Whenever you find yourself in fear or stress, it won't help to try to block it out of your mind or beat yourself up for it! Rather, you must remember, "God has not given me this spirit of fear or stress—it's not from Him, therefore I need to use spiritual weapons of warfare to break free from this fiery dart of the enemy!"

Your Spiritual Weapons of Warfare

Now back to my story—that's exactly what I did that morning. After God showed me the root stronghold messages or lies that I was believing about myself and God, I used my spiritual weapons of warfare to break free from those lies. I will go into more detail in Chapter 4, but in order to get through this story, I'll give you the quick highlights now. First, I confessed my fear and the lies that I was believing as sin; second, I forgave anyone who had hurt me—and in this case it was this man for declaring all of these horrific things upon my family, my friends who had introduced me to him, and my family who fired the original arrows at my heart with these messages attached; third, in the name of Jesus I commanded the spirits of fear, rejection, and abandonment to go; and fourth, I cancelled the authority I had given the enemy by agreeing with those thoughts that were telling me I'm unprotected, that God's abandoned me, and every other lie listed above.

It's only when we use spiritual weapons of warfare to cut the ropes (that give the enemy a handle in our lives) that we are free to hear from God in a very personal way that speaks truth and healing to our hearts. So many times we complain that God is not there, He's distant, He's not listening, He won't speak to us, or that He speaks to everyone else (the more spiritual ones) but not to us! We experience this because we are hanging on to these ropes that block us from hearing God speak to us! Picture yourself holding on to one end of the rope, and the enemy holding on to the other.

Remember, God *always* wants to reveal truth to you. He never hides or operates in darkness. First John 1:5 tells us that *"God is light and in Him is no darkness at all!"* The enemy always wants to keep you from the truth and always wants you to blame God for what he's doing! So let's stop blaming God for not speaking to us;

instead, let's get busy using our spiritual weapons of warfare to cut the ropes or handles we've given the enemy so that we *can* hear from God. Do I hear an *amen* out there?

God Speaks Through the Fear

Oh the story, yes, let's get back to my story. I cut those ropes, and this is what God showed me. First, He told me to focus on what I *do know*, not on what I don't know. What this man said was not "gospel truth," it was not set in stone. I *don't* know for sure that what he said will happen, so I shouldn't focus on that, but rather on what I *do know* about God.

Why He Died

What I do know is that He died to have intimate relationship with me (and you). In fact, He took death upon Himself, even though there was nothing more contaminating than death, even though He was equal to God (see Phil. 2:5–9), even though He is on the throne (see Rev. 4), and even though He is coming back as King of Kings and Lord of Lords (see Rev. 19)! Why? Because He wanted you so badly! He's not going to go to those extreme lengths for you to be with Him only to abandon you and no longer want to be with you—just because it's the end times! He wants to have intimate relationship with you every minute of the day! He never changes! He's the same yesterday, today, and forever (see Heb. 13:8)! He desires the same level of intimacy with you no matter what the times!

Others' Faces on Him

He also showed me that I was putting my dad and brothers' faces on Him! God does not scowl at me with disgust, look down on me, become annoyed by my very presence, view me as a pest, have no interest in me, shut me out, or stay behind an impenetrable wall like they did. He loves being with me, enjoys me, can't wait to spend time with me, and misses me when I am focused on anything else other than Him! He delights in spending time with me—just the opposite of how everyone in my family felt about me when I was growing up!

Never Give Up!

He reminded me ever so lovingly (when God convicts it brings us into forward motion; when the enemy condemns it always stops us or takes us backward) what we do now *does* matter in the future. It is never God's will for us to give up or to hide out under the covers until He returns. Those thoughts and inclinations are never from God. The Parable of the Talents (see Luke 19:10–28, Matt. 25:14–30) makes it clear what happens to those who think it's best to hide out until He returns! The one who basically "gave up" and did nothing until the Master returned was considered wicked and worthless and was cast into outer darkness.

It's Always Worthwhile

However, the Master (Jesus) rewarded those who used the talents or gifts that they had been given. It is *always* worthwhile to move forward in righteousness, even when you think there is nothing you can do that could possibly make a difference or that things are too far gone. Giving up and being passive and apathetic are schemes of the enemy to keep you doing nothing so that evil *can* reign. Fear only increases the enemy's reign over your hearts and in this world. What you do now *does* matter, not only today but in the future. We want to be vessels through whom God accomplishes His purposes for such a time as this. We want to look forward to rewards when we rule and reign with Him in the Millennium!

Righteousness Lives On

"The Milleni-what?" The Millennium! That 1,000-year period after Jesus returns to earth (see Rev. 20). You have a very exciting future to look forward to, and what you do *now* for righteousness will continue on into the Millennium. However, you'll just have to wait until Chapter 5 to find out more about the Millennium or else I'll really get off track here and never finish my story!

Prayer Works!

Last, but in no way least, God reminded me that no one knows exactly what will happen in our country, but we *do* know that prayer is our most powerful weapon of warfare. Prayer works, and throughout the Bible it has changed the course of world events! Look at these examples from Scripture:

> *Return to the Lord...He is gracious and merciful, slow to anger, and of great kindness; and He relents from doing harm. Who knows if He will turn and relent, and leave a blessing* (Joel 2:13-14).

> *[Abraham] said, "Let not the Lord be angry, and I will speak but once more: Suppose ten should be found there?" And He said, "I will not destroy it for the sake of ten"* (Genesis 18:32).

> *Then Moses pleaded with the Lord his God, and said, "... Turn from Your fierce wrath, and relent from this harm to your people." ...So the Lord relented from the harm which He said He would do to His people* (Exodus 32:11-12,14).

> *So I sought for a man among them who would make a wall, and stand in the gap before Me on behalf of the land, that I should not destroy it; but I found no one* (Ezekiel 22:30).

I said: "O Lord God, forgive, I pray!" ...So the Lord relented concerning this. ...I said, "O Lord God, cease, I pray!" ...So the Lord relented concerning this (Amos 7:2-3,5-6).

Our country is not a "done deal"; we must pray for repentance, revival, for the spirit of deception to be bound, and for eyes and hearts to be open to receive truth!

Let's Go Forward

Ever since I experienced being "Paralyzed by Fear," and all that God showed me through it, I have felt compelled to share my story so that it might mobilize *you* out of fear, stress, frustration, anger, passivity, or apathy in these end times! I want you to be freed from the enemy's grip to enjoy the blessing and the privilege of partnering with God to release His power, plans, and purposes and to experience all that God has for you in these exciting times. You have been chosen for a very specific and powerful purpose, so let's go forward and explore the anchors that God has given you to stand strong and resolute, unwavering and unshaken during these turbulent, uncertain end times.

Chapter 2

Object of His Affection

What is *the* key to standing strong and unshaken in these uncertain, turbulent times? The answer is *intimacy with God!*

What Is Intimacy with God?

Intimacy. The word itself is loaded with so many different meanings! How in the world do you define intimacy with God? I'd like to try by asking you to think back with me for a moment to your first crush back in elementary school or your first boyfriend/ girlfriend. Do you remember how you felt about that person? Did you think about them all throughout the day? Talk to your friends about them? Look forward to being with them? Did you feel special because they liked you?

I sure remember mine; even though it's been over 40 years now, it seems those "first crushes and loves" are forever etched in our memories.

When I picture school days, I see hallways packed with noisy students and classrooms full of uncomfortable wooden desks organized in straight rows. Tables weren't clustered into groups or u-shapes to foster teamwork as they are now. Teamwork was not yet a buzzword in the '60s and '70s! I remember passing notes to friends during class every time the teacher looked away; that was our form of texting in those days!

And what was the subject of all those little notes strategically passed across classrooms and hallways? Oftentimes, it was boys! When we liked someone, that's all we could think about! They were the object of our attention and our affection. We wrote our first names with their last names all over our notebooks (as practice just in case we got married); we talked about them all the time; we beamed with joy in the feeling of being liked, desired, valued, special, set apart, sought after, and that they viewed us as attractive and beautiful. Every song reminded us of them; even though we were too young to fully understand the words to the song—somehow they all related to that crush!

As I got older, I would wait by the phone for their call (before the days of answering machines or voicemail), so excited to talk with them. Their call would take priority over everyone else's (this was back in the day when couples actually talked on the phone instead of texted). I couldn't wait to be with them, talk with them, share with them, listen to them, hear their voice. And like most girls, I tried to picture my wedding day—what will the dress look like, who will be in the wedding, where will it be, etc. No matter how young or old, girls delight in thinking about that glorious day in the future when they will be able to spend the rest of their lives with the one they love.

To sum it up, that person was the object of our affection and our attention, and we were the object of theirs (hopefully)! I believe God created us to have these kinds of desires and emotions, but to have them for Him first. The truth is, you are the object of God's affection and attention, and *He* wants to be the object of yours!

The Object of God's Affection and Attention

How incredible is that? *You* are the object of affection and attention of the God who created the universe, stretched out the heavens, formed the foundations of the earth and the spirit of man within him; who is seated on the throne emanating with diamond-like glory, fire, thunder and lightning; is all-powerful; and who will come back to destroy all the kings of the nations and establish righteousness throughout the earth. He, in turn, desires to be the object of your affection and attention, which might sound very similar to what I described above:

"I talk about God all the time. I think about God all the time. I beam with joy in the feeling of being liked, desired, wanted, valued, special, set apart, sought after by God and that He views me as beautiful (even in my weakness) and enjoys being with me. I am so excited to talk with God; His call (voice) takes priority over everyone else's. I can't wait to spend time alone with God, share with Him, listen to Him, hear His voice; I delight in thinking about that glorious day in the future when I will be able to spend the rest of my life with Him."

Head vs. Heart Knowledge

Intimacy with God is not head knowledge of God. It is heart knowledge of who He is, His incredible love for you, what He's done for you, how He sees you, and His wisdom and power that becomes *real* and *alive* to you all throughout the day.

Even in the book of Daniel we see that intimacy with God is the key to standing strong in uncertain times. When he prophesied future times of persecution, believers falling away, and the defilement of all things holy to God, he stated that the people who *know* their God (know Him *intimately*, that is, not just with head knowledge) would stand strong and be used mightily by God! *"The people who know their God shall be strong, and carry out great exploits"* (Dan. 11:32).

When I think about intimacy with God, what comes to mind is experiencing a close connection with God that impacts every aspect of my life:

- I'm thinking what He thinks.

- I'm feeling what He feels.

- I'm speaking what He says.

- All throughout the day I'm dwelling on who He is, how much He loves me, what He's done for me, how He sees me, how much He enjoys and desires to be with me every minute of the day.

- I'm allowing His love and how He sees me to permeate every thought, emotion, attitude, word, and action of my day.

- I'm acting upon the wisdom of His Word and hearing His voice guide me.

- I'm aware of Him working in every little detail of my life.

- I'm seeing Him as my perfect bridegroom, not just intellectually but emotionally and experientially.

- I'm aligning with His heart in all things.

Let's take a look at the four major reasons why intimacy with God is your key anchor for standing strong and unshaken in these uncertain end times.

1) Intimacy with God Is Your Primary Purpose in Life

Life is really much simpler than we all make it out to be. What do I mean by that? We make life so stressful and complicated by focusing on all we have to get done each day, the fears and the "what ifs," all of the things and people we wish we could change in our lives, families, communities, government, and world in general. Then, on top of that we add all of the technology that was intended to somehow simplify our lives. Instead, it has made us 100 times busier and more stressed out as a culture than we were 20 to 30 years ago! It used to be that when work was over at 5 P.M. or 6 P.M., it was over. Now we can never get away from it thanks to our modern conveniences of email, text, and social media that carry with them the expectation of immediate response! It seems we are "on call" 24/7 to everyone and anyone's request.

However, it is important to remember that the overload we all feel is *not* from God. He doesn't make things complicated and high pressure for us. He's not a God of confusion, but of clarity (see 1 Cor. 14:33). His yoke is easy and His burden is light (see Matt. 11:30). God actually desires to simplify our lives, and contrary to many misperceptions we have of Him, He's *for* us; He's not out to crush us!

The "One Thing"

In fact, He's made it clear that you only need to focus on *one thing!* In Luke 10:41-42, Jesus says, *"you are worried and troubled about many things.* (That accurately describes me, how about you?) *But **one thing** is needed."* That "one thing" is intimacy with God, and again, it's *the* key to standing strong in uncertain end times.

Just imagine how much simpler your life would be if when you woke up in the morning you said to yourself (or better yet out loud), "Praise God! I only have to focus on *one thing* today!"

If you're anything like me, that is not my default, auto-pilot mode when I wake up in the morning. On the contrary, when I first get up in the morning, my mind defaults to thinking about all that I need to get done, not only that day but in the days and months ahead! My natural tendency is to stress with negative, anxious thoughts, such as: "I'm *so* tired; it's not fair I had to stay up so late with my daughter's homework last night. What are we going to do about this? Maybe we should switch schools; oh, I need to look into homeschooling, but I have no time to do that, ugh. I'm not going to get these chapters done on time; I'm behind in my husband's expense reports. I wish I didn't have a PT appointment today," etc., etc., followed by, "How am I going to have the energy to make it through the day? What if we need to sell this house, how would I ever have time to pack up? I'm so behind in emails, I'll never catch up!" Then, I turn on the news and see the stock market crashing or terrorist attacks. My thoughts move to "Ugh, we should have done something with our investments; that reminds me, we still didn't get emergency food; what if terrorism strikes here, should I cancel my plans to fly? Should I even leave my house today?" Does any of this sound familiar to you, or is it just me?

"To-do" Lists Become God!

I have post-its all throughout the house so that regardless of whether I'm in the kitchen, bedroom, putting on makeup, walking on the treadmill, you name it, I can add things to my many to-do lists. But wait, aren't to-do lists a good thing? Yes, but before long they and our circumstances can become "God" because anything that we dwell on and set our minds and hearts upon becomes a god or a false idol in our lives! We get deceived into thinking that our purpose each day is to get our to-do list done. For me it's to get this book done, this teaching done, this blog written, my daughter's situations worked out, my husband's work done, etc., but those things are *not* my primary purpose in life, and *your* to-do list is not your purpose either!

I spent the first 28 years of my life searching for my purpose and the meaning of life. I went deep. I wracked my brain and heart all those years reading every psychology, philosophy, spiritual, and new age book I could get my hands on. I moved to California thinking I would find truth there and tried every career, religion, and philosophy that I possibly could. I spent endless hours and years analyzing, pondering, reading—all to no avail. And yet the answer was so simple, it's only *one thing*—intimacy with God—that is our purpose for living!

Just to Know Him

A few years ago, a friend of mine from high school passed away from ovarian cancer. It was the first person I had been close to in high school who died from cancer. Suddenly it didn't seem like a disease that could not affect me, or someone my age, or someone like me—it became all too real, all too up close and personal.

I went into a bit of a depressive spiral and started to question—why are we here anyway? What's the point if we just end up dying due to these terrible diseases? So we work hard at our jobs, for our families, even in developing strong and healthy relationships with our family and friends, all to just eventually lose them? I'll never forget what God spoke to my heart that day in His still small voice. Remember when God speaks to you, it's always with a loving tone to move you forward, not to condemn you, put you down, or cause you to halt or give up.

He simply said *"to know Me."* You are here, your purpose in life, your purpose for getting up each day is *"to know Me."* Eventually those three words evolved into what I now call "growing in intimacy with God." That is my sole purpose for living. Now, of course you are called to your families, jobs, churches, communities, friends, etc., but all of that has to be an overflow from first experiencing intimacy with God.

Intimacy First

Intimacy with Him is really all He wants from you; it's the *one thing* that He asks of you. It's why He died for you. Once I was feeling very burdened with all of the ministry work I needed to get done, and I certainly wasn't experiencing that "His yoke was easy and His burden was light." As I confessed my feelings of frustration to the Lord, He spoke these words to my heart: "I died to have (intimate) relationship with you, not for you to work for Me." His primary purpose in dying for you was because *He* so intensely desired intimate relationship with you, not so that you could work for Him or be a good Christian.

He knows that if you have intimate relationship with Him, everything else will flow out of it—the work, the service, the love—and you won't have to strive; it will flow naturally and freely!

God the Task Master

However, if intimacy with God does not come first, then you will do everything on your own strength and in your own human love instead of with God's strength and love. You might put someone else's face on God and start believing that He's a slave driver or a task master who is constantly putting pressure on you to do more and love more. You may then feel like you just can't measure up to His expectations and standards for you, and end up being burned out, resenting Him, and feeling distant from Him.

We can even feel ashamed before Him and hide out thinking that He's mad at us or disappointed in us for not being perfect or that we have to "get it together" before we can feel close to Him again. We accuse Him of being impossible to please and feel we just can't be the "good Christians" He wants us to be. We feel weighed down and believe that the burden is from God. We get physically exhausted, and we may even develop diseases from the resentment and anger that always lies just below the surface. We have no joy in what we are doing and we don't look any different from the person who doesn't know God. We are burned out, stressed, fearful, and frustrated. Can you relate? That pretty much describes me on the days that I forget that my purpose, the *one thing* that I *have* to do and focus on that day, is intimacy with Him.

When your primary purpose for getting up each morning, for going through each day is to experience intimacy with God, that is an anchor that will keep you strong, steady, and unshaken regardless of your circumstances or what's happening in the world around you. In Chapters 3 and 4, we'll explore how to grow in intimacy with God as well as how to break free from anything that blocks intimacy with Him.

2) Intimacy with God Is the Only Thing You Cannot Lose

The second reason intimacy with God is so important for standing unshaken in these uncertain end times is because it's the *only* thing that cannot be taken away from you. It's the *only* thing that cannot change!

Relationships Change

First, we've all experienced change in relationships—people can disappoint us, hurt us, let us down, and make mistakes (no one is perfect). They can even "push our buttons," and then we end up dwelling on them all day. For example, someone speaks to me in a derogatory or frustrated tone which pushes my button, and then I'm angry, shut down, or feeling like a "bad girl" the rest of the day. When our mood or our happiness depends upon other people, we will always be going up and down like a roller coaster!

Circumstances Change

Second, our circumstances can change—my best laid out plans for the day continue to be interrupted, and so I'm dwelling on everything that I'm *not* getting done. As a result, I'm frustrated, stressed out, angry, and short with others. Perhaps I'm in a great mood until I hear that things look bad for my husband's company or that my daughter had a rough time at school. Then I end up feeling down, discouraged, negative, and fearful for the rest of the day.

God Never Changes

Whenever our mood or feelings are dependent upon anything other than God, that circumstance or person has become God to us and is on the throne of our lives. God always gently reminds me—"You've forgotten that I'm the only thing that can't change. Everything else in your life can change at any moment! You're looking for your happiness to be based upon everything going as you planned, or people responding the way you think they should, and this will never happen because only I cannot change!" There is no variation or turning with Him! (See James 1:17.) *"For I am the Lord, I do not change"* (Mal. 3:6). Whenever I'm disappointed in a person, organization, or circumstance, God shows me that I was looking to them to be who only God can be or to do what only God can do!

Everything and anything can be taken away from us—jobs, religious freedoms, finances, health, relationships—except for our intimate relationship with God. Once we finally accept this fact, then we will not rely upon anything else but our intimacy with Him to determine our happiness, mood, joy, and emotions.

Intimacy Is Not an Option

As these end times become even more uncertain and most likely more difficult, intimacy with God will no longer be an option or a "nice to know" teaching for those hardcore Christians who have all the time in the world to do Bible studies, for the "super spiritual," or for women only! It simply won't be enough to have only "head knowledge" about God. It won't cut it to attend church just because it feels good and has a fun social environment. You are going to need moment by moment intimacy, true encounters with the person of Jesus, not just an intellectual belief in Him. Your very survival will depend upon it in these end times—spiritually, emotionally, mentally, and physically.

Practice for the Future

We're talking life or death here! He's giving you "practice" *now* in drawing close to Him so that you will be able to stand strong and unshaken as things continue to heat up even more. I believe very strongly that God really wants you to get this point *now* before it's too late, while there's still time to get it! View the daily struggles in your lives as practices for the future. They are opportunities to focus on what you *do* know about God and His character. Otherwise, you will fall prey to the enemy during uncertain times. You will blame God for your circumstances, become fearful, stressed, frustrated, confused, angry, unforgiving—and look just like everyone else who is in the world. You will block God's light and His purposes through you.

If the stressors of daily life from unexpected interruptions or someone pushing your button, rejecting you, or disappointing you throws you off now, how will you be able to stand against the big things? You watch the news and wonder what could happen next? Could terrorism and ISIS hit here? Could someone I love get randomly shot and killed or wounded? Could I get in a car accident? Could the economy collapse? Could I lose my job? Could I lose my marriage? Could my teenager or millennial go wayward from the Lord? Could I lose my religious freedoms? Freedom of speech? Right to bear arms? What if I can no longer get to or afford food in the stores? What if earthquakes and natural disasters destroy all that I have? What if I get sick? What if there's a nuclear war?

At any given moment, your entire life could change and anything could be taken away from you—anything, that is, except for your intimacy with God. The good news is that He *always* desires intimacy with you. *You* are the only one who can cause a loss of intimacy with God. This means you need to start growing in intimacy with Him as well as becoming more aware of and dealing with whatever blocks intimacy *now* before it's too late.

Make it a habit when you wake up in the morning, starting *now*, to focus on that *one thing* you have to do that day—growing in intimacy with God. If you can do it *now* with the usual ups and downs of daily life, you'll be able to remain strong no matter how uncertain the times become in the future.

3) Intimacy with God Will Keep You from Deception

Think for just a moment about the people in your life you consider to be acquaintances versus those with whom you would say you have a heart connection. What are the primary differences between those two types of relationships in your life? Typically, one of the major differences is that you *know more* about those with whom you have a deeper relationship.

Now in using the word *know*, I don't mean you know just the surface facts or how the person presents themselves in a social setting; I mean you know the real, true person inside (without the outer mask or façade). You know about their family, their background, the culture in which they grew up. You have access to what is on their mind and heart, you understand what motivates them, what drives them, what their goals and passions are, and you want to partner or join with them in their journey of fulfilling their dreams and passions. Well, it's exactly the same way with God. A critical aspect of experiencing true intimacy with God is knowing who He truly is, *as He has revealed Himself*, that is.

The "Falling Away"

The problem we have with knowing *who He is* is that we, the church, and the world have defined and described God in the way that *we* want Him to be. In other words, we focus on one or maybe a few of His characteristics that we like and that serve us well, and we ignore the rest. The serious dangers of doing this are twofold: 1) we can't truly experience and grow in intimacy with God (or with anyone) when we only desire to know certain parts of them; and 2) it opens us up to be extremely vulnerable to deception, which will eventually lead to "falling away" from the faith. "What? Falling away? No way! That could never happen to me," you might be saying!

I understand, but let me explain. I sincerely believe that if we do not have true intimacy with God and experience heart knowledge of *all* of His characteristics as He has defined Himself (not as we have defined Him), we will be among those who are deceived and who might possibly fall away. Jesus tell us:

For false christs and false prophets will rise and show great signs and wonders to deceive, if possible, even the elect. See, I have told you beforehand (Matthew 24:24-25; see also Mark 13:22).

Well, Jesus knows what He's talking about, and so I'm going to believe that this will happen one way or another because He said so!

In 2 Thessalonians 2:3, we are told that "the falling away" will occur before the second coming of Jesus:

Let no one deceive you by any means; for that Day (Jesus' return) *will not come unless the falling away comes first, and the man of sin* (antichrist) *is revealed, the son of perdition.*

Furthermore, 1 Timothy 4:1 says that "in latter times some will depart from the faith, giving heed to **deceiving spirits and doctrines of demons**."

The Tidal Wave Has Hit!

There is such a powerful deception coming upon the church, I can actually picture a tidal wave that will take over many before they even know what hit them. But wait, I see that the tidal wave has already begun to swell and there are already many who are deceived! Unless we start experiencing intimacy with God now (as He has revealed Himself), there will only be a small remnant of believers left who are not deceived and stay true to God's Word.

Why do I believe there will be such widespread deception? First, because I already see it happening within the church. Believers are questioning and making excuses for God's Word based on the messages they are receiving and buying into from our culture. Abortion is understandable depending upon the circumstances;

there's nothing really wrong with homosexuality and same-sex marriage because love wins and it's not hurting anyone. Sex outside of marriage is to be expected; after all, people are waiting until they are older now to get married, so purity is just not realistic when you're in your 20s and 30s. The Bible was written when people got married at age 13 for goodness' sake! Tolerance and social justice come first over the salvation message, and besides, all religions lead to the same God ultimately; do they really need Jesus to get to heaven if they are sincere in their belief in God—as they have defined Him?

God "Defined"

And that last phrase—*as they have defined Him*—is exactly where the window opens wide for deception. Our culture has defined God in its own terms—someone who should be there to help us when there's a natural disaster, terror attack, or school shooting, but not needed or wanted at any other time. The church has defined God, and we as individuals have defined God—He is Love and only Love, He exists to meet our needs, He's our personal shopper, He's our best friend, He gets us into heaven but until then we can do what we want and still get in as long as we said the "sinners prayer," etc.

The problem with all of these definitions of God is that they are based upon one or maybe two of His attributes, not *all* of them! Yes, God is love, but He is also *Truth, Holy, Sovereign, Righteous, Just, Eternal, Omniscient, Omnipotent, Omnipresent, Never Changing*, and He's all of these *at the same time!* He doesn't switch from one characteristic to another at different times depending upon our needs. He never changes.

> *Jesus Christ is the same yesterday, today, and forever* (Hebrews 13:8).

the Father of lights, with whom there is no variation or shadow of turning (James 1:17).

For I am the Lord, I do not change (Malachi 3:6).

So if we are only holding on to the attribute of love and none of the others, of course same-sex marriage and homosexuality will look *good*, because after all what could be wrong about people living in love? Of course an emphasis on tolerance, feeding the poor, cleaning up the environment, and social justice will look *good*; these are all good things, but apart from allegiance to Jesus the *cause itself* becomes God. The cause—social justice, for example—is worshiped and adored rather than Jesus on the throne.

God "Re-defined"

Of course Jesus is our friend and desires to meet our needs, but He is also holy! This is the topic of a future book, but just to give you a sneak preview:

1. When you explore Leviticus, the sacrifices, the laws of ritual purification and clean and unclean; when you study Solomon and Herod's temples, as well as Ezekiel's future Millennial temple—its practices, laws, and rituals of the priests—you come away with a clear picture of God's holiness, love, and mercy working together! His love was always making a way for us to draw near to Him, while mercy kept anything remotely related to death out of His presence so that it didn't burn up from His holiness!

2. When you study the throne room scene in Revelation 4, Jesus is revealed shining forth in unapproachable light like a diamond, with fiery eyes, with a voice like thunder and lightning. All

throughout Scripture, when prophets were given a vision of Jesus or God the Father, fire was always in the description, and their immediate response was to *fall down* on their faces before Him. Is that our response when we come into God's presence in prayer or in a worship service, or are we thinking about what we have to get done that day or what we need from Him?

When you start out your day with a focus on the throne room, it puts everything else in perspective! You are reminded that He is holy! Yes, He is your friend and bridegroom, but He is also on the throne worthy to be praised! Your heart cries out to worship Him throughout the day, in awe of who He is! Suddenly your circumstances do not seem so big in comparison to the revelation of Jesus in the throne room.

Whenever our focus or study is only on one or two of God's attributes, excluding the others, that's when deception comes creeping in. The coming deceptions are going to have the appearance of *good things!* Otherwise, if they were blatantly bad, they would not deceive! Deceptions are not going to come from someone who has horns and carries a pitchfork! The nature of the deception that is rapidly coming upon us is *going to be in the name of Jesus, and it's going to have prayer and worship and the Bible attached to it!* Beware, the spirits behind it will be deceiving and the doctrines demonic (see 1 Tim. 4:1)!

However, when you study, focus on, and experience God *as He has revealed Himself,* you won't be deceived by teachings that are based upon only one attribute of God, and you won't fall away from the faith. On the contrary, you will be able to stand strong, unshaken in the face of deception, continuing to release and accomplish His end-times purposes on this earth.

4) Intimacy with God Will Keep You Strong in Times of Persecution

Misperceptions of Persecution

Every day in the news we hear about believers in the Middle East and Africa facing terrible persecution by ISIS, Iran, and other Islamic nations. Have you ever thought about how you would respond if you knew you would lose your job, home, everything you owned, or even your life for admitting that you were a Christian? It's such a sobering and convicting thought, it seems that our response has been to create two separate doctrines of Christianity. One for us here in the U.S., and one for those in other countries. Somehow, persecution is only a part of "their" Christian experience, but it's not a part of ours. This belief system may have worked for us in the past, but I believe it's short lived. Christians are soon going to be persecuted in this country as well.

The faithful, undeceived Christians will be seen as the only ones who are "standing in the way of love and peace—God's ultimate plan for this earth." They will actually be viewed as haters, as enemies of God—*God as the world has defined Him*, that is. These intolerant Christians, guilty of hate crimes, will need to be punished and removed from society. It's happening already with job firings and lawsuits against those who will not support a same-sex lifestyle.

So how are *you* going to *stand strong* and unshaken in the face of this persecution?

Seeing Yourself as God Sees You

The only way you will be able to remain strong and unshaken in the face of criticism, rejection, and ultimately persecution is by seeing yourself as God sees you! But first, in order to see yourself as God sees you, you have to see God for who *He* truly is. We will only know who *we* are when we first know who *God* is! As I explained in the last section, that means experiencing heart knowledge of all the attributes He has revealed about Himself, not just a select few.

When you grasp how *holy* and *loving* and *merciful* He is all at the same time—it gives you an incredibly deep appreciation for what Jesus did for you on the cross. We have become so casual about the fact that Jesus died for us, but when we truly understand and know who He is *as He has defined Himself* (e.g., in the Temple practices or the Revelation throne room scene), not as the world, church, or we have defined Him, then we are utterly in awe of what He did for us.

The same God who is so holy that nothing even remotely associated with death could come near His manifest presence in the temple actually *took death upon Himself because He wanted you so intensely*, because you're so *valuable* to Him! What does that say about your worth, value, identity, and security? It's off the charts! When you picture that throne room scene in Revelation 4 described with diamonds, emeralds, fire, and a sea of glass surrounded by nonstop worship and adoration and elders falling on their faces because He is worthy to receive all glory, honor, and power—and then realize that the same God who is worthy of 24/7 praise and worship would become a man and die for you because He wanted you so badly, because you're so valuable to Him—what does that say about your worth, value, identity, and security? What does it say about how He sees you that you can enter into the Holy of Holies at any time, a place where the High Priest was required to be and do everything perfectly or else he would die?

God's Insane Love

I call it an "insane love," and He did it all because He wanted intimate relationship with you! Getting that truth down into your heart is *the* key to healing the strongholds of being unwanted, worthless, or fearing rejection and disapproval! I can proclaim this with much boldness and confidence because I personally have experienced deep healing of those very strongholds in my own life through these truths.

It's the heart knowledge of being so intensely desired, wanted, accepted and valued by God that you are going to need to stand strong and unshaken in the face of criticism, rejection, and persecution. Otherwise, you will be controlled by fears of rejection, disapproval, not being liked or accepted, or being criticized.

We are all human and we all have the need to be liked, accepted, have friends, and feel wanted. I've never met anyone who actually enjoys being rejected! It's the way we were all wired and designed by God! But again, those needs can only be fully met by God Himself and by seeing ourselves as He sees us.

First you must connect with *all* facets of God's heart, and then ask Him to show you, "In light of who You are and what You have done for me, what does that say about me? What does it say about my worth, value, identity, acceptance, and security?" Only then will you be able to see yourself as He sees you, which is an anchor you will need to stand strong in these times, to remain unshaken in the face of persecution.

Do you find that you're still controlled at times by fear of rejection, criticism, disapproval, not being liked and accepted? I know I am; we all are. Do you fear that you will not be able to stand strong in the face of criticism of your faith, rejection, and ultimately persecution? Fear not, because in the next few chapters we'll explore how to grow in intimacy with God, as well as how to break free from barriers to intimacy, such as fear.

Hopefully by now you see that intimacy with God is the *one thing* you need to focus on each day—and it's the reason He died for you! It's your very purpose for living; it's the only thing that can't be taken away from you; it will keep you from being deceived; and it will enable you to stand strong in the face of criticism, rejection, and persecution. Truly, intimacy with God is your key anchor for staying *unshaken* in these uncertain end times.

Chapter 3

Dwelling in His House

The Simple Life

"I don't believe in frettin' and grievin'...give me the simple life. Just serve me tomatoes; and mashed potatoes; Give me the simple life...free from the care and strife...yes, indeed-y; I like the simple life.

Remember that song from *Father of the Bride Part II*? Oh, how we all yearn for the simple life! We tend to think it was lost in yesteryear, never again to be found in this crazy, stressed-out, turbulent world in which we live. However, I believe that we *can* experience it now, even in these uncertain end times! It's a lie of the enemy that being loaded down with burdens and in bondage to stress, pressures, and fears is just a normal part of daily life until we get to heaven.

Only One Thing

As I emphasized in Chapter 2, focusing on just one thing—intimacy with God—is the key to experiencing this simpler, less stressful, unshaken life *right now!*

You are worried and troubled about so many things. But one thing is needed (Luke 10:41-42).

One thing I have desired of the Lord, that will I seek: that I may dwell in the house of the Lord all the days of my life, to behold the beauty of the Lord, and to inquire in His temple (Psalms 27:4).

Intimacy with Him is the *one thing* that He desires of you. It's the reason He died for you. Remember those words He spoke so clearly to my heart—"I died to have (intimate) relationship with you, not for you to work for Me." He desires close relationship with you every minute of the day, no matter what you are doing.

I hope you have begun to remind yourself every morning (especially when those thoughts flood in about all you have to get done and all that is worrying you) that you only need to focus on *one thing* that day! If you haven't, I strongly encourage you to—that is, if you really want to stand strong and unshaken no matter what is going on in your life circumstances or in the world.

Intimacy with God has to be your primary purpose and goal for each day—not to get your to-do list done, not even to take care of your family or minister to others. He just wants to be with you— He wants *you*, not what you can *do* for Him. Besides, you'll find that when you are experiencing intimacy with God, everything else will fall into place and it will be accomplished out of *His* love, wisdom, and power—not your own efforts to make things happen.

Intimacy Is a Choice

Focusing on just *one thing* brings me such relief compared to dwelling on the hundreds of things I tend to focus on each day! When I remind myself each morning, it instantly transforms my mood and my day. However, did you notice that I have to *remind* myself? Intimacy with God is not something you just wake up with in the morning! It doesn't blow in with the wind; sometimes you feel it and sometimes you don't. You are not passive receivers who sometimes "get it" and sometimes don't. You have to make a conscious choice to focus on and grow in intimacy with God *each day*—actually, every moment of the day. I can't emphasize this point enough—it's really all He's asking of you each day, and as I detailed in Chapter 2 it's your very purpose for living, it's the only thing that can't change, it will keep you from deception, and it will give you the identity and security to stand strong in the face of persecution.

If I asked the "average" Christian whether they desire greater intimacy in their relationship with God, I would guess that the vast majority would respond, "*Yes!*" Most of us long for a closer relationship with God, but often we feel that it's out of our reach. We might feel intimacy with God is reserved only for the spiritual elite, the "super spiritual" who have time to pray and read the Word all day, or for those who were just born with a more "direct line" to heaven. However, God is no respecter of persons!

> *In truth I perceive that God shows no partiality* (Acts 10:34).

> *For there is no partiality with God* (Romans 2:11).

He passionately desires to draw near in intimacy with you! Again, He died for you because He wanted you so intensely and you were so valuable to Him! Now if the desire of God's heart is to have deep intimacy with you, this means that experiencing it is just as possible for you as it is for someone you may perceive is more worthy, just made that way, or has more time!

What to Do?

Next, if I asked the "average" Christian what they believe they need to *do* in order to grow in intimacy with God, I would guess that most feel they need to *do* more things! These may include attending more Bible studies and retreats; spending more time in the Word and in prayer; doing more missions work or going into full-time ministry—all of which require significant adjustments in lifestyle. Now granted, doing these things would have a positive impact on your relationship with God. But what is the primary way you grow in intimacy with God? I believe it is by bringing Him into the moment-by-moment thoughts, emotions, words, and attitudes of your daily life.

I strongly believe that *now* is the time for us to get this! Out of His mercy and grace, God is giving us time now to practice before things get even worse in our world. It needs to become normal routine for us to wake up in the morning and focus on that *one thing*, knowing that His desire to be with us is the only thing that *can't* change. If we can do that now with the usual ups, downs, and stresses of our lives, then we will remain unshaken no matter how uncertain the times. As my husband always says, "If you don't do it in the practice, you won't do it in the game!"

Intimacy and Football

Speaking of game, as I prayed for a way to describe how to grow in intimacy with God, quite unexpectedly, the picture of a football game came to mind. In our goal of experiencing intimacy with Him, we must operate like a football team! That is, we must make both offensive *and* defensive moves.

Now, I'm no expert on sports and neither was my dad. However, when I was 11 years old, he took me to my first pro game with the Cleveland Browns and taught me the basics. The times when I felt a connection with my dad were few and far between when I was young, and so this special memory is still etched upon my heart. I became an avid fan of pro football, collecting stickers of every NFL player (we earned them from buying gasoline in the early '70s!) and watching all of the Browns and Dolphins games. I must confess that I cheered for the Dolphins because in sixth grade I liked a boy who wore a Dolphins jacket!

Back to the point, how does a football game relate to intimacy with God? Through this picture, the Lord showed me that "offensive moves" are those which enable us to make progress down the field toward our goal of greater intimacy with Him.

However, just as with football, you have an opposing team—Satan and his demons—whose goal is to block you, tackle you, and take you in the opposite direction down the field, away from your goal of intimacy with God. "Defensive moves" are those you need to make in order to break through these barriers or blocks to intimacy so that you are free to make offensive moves in the right direction—toward greater intimacy with God.

Therefore, to truly grow deeper in intimacy with God, you need to actively pursue and commit to making both offensive *and* defensive moves.

First, I'll describe the *offensive* moves—what you *can* do to grow in intimacy with Him. Then, in Chapter 4, I'll address the *defensive* moves.

Offensive Moves for Growing in Intimacy with God

1. Dwell on Him throughout the day.

2. Thank Him out loud throughout the day.

3. Connect with His heart.

Dwell on Him Throughout the Day:
What He Has Done for You

- How much He wants to be with you

- How much He desires you

- How much He values you

A key ingredient of my prayer time and of my dwelling on Him throughout the day is a constant focus on what Jesus did when He took death upon Himself to be with me. This communicates more powerfully than anything else how intensely He desired me, valued me, and wants to be with me at all times. I've found that having a picture of the Temple in my mind helps me to maintain this focus. "The Temple?" you might ask. "What could an ancient, Old Testament temple possibly have to do with intimacy with Jesus? Isn't that the law and aren't we no longer under the law?" Oh, how the enemy wants to rip you off from anything that will draw you into intimacy with God!

Leviticus Comes Alive!

What comes to your mind when you think of the book of Leviticus? Sleeping, or perhaps outdated, irrelevant detail that is "not for today"? Well, in my opinion and experience, the book of Leviticus is one of the most powerful books in the Bible for communicating who God is, how He sees you, and for healing your heart. There is *so* much about the sacrificial system of the tabernacle and temples, their offerings, sacrifices, services, priests' rituals, laws of clean and unclean, ritual purification, etc. that has brought deep healing to the strongholds of my heart and has *greatly* increased my intimacy with God! Be watching for another book focused on this topic, but for now, I will give you the highlights.

For example, have you ever thought about the fact that every law of ritual purification—whether it had to do with childbirth, menstruation, emissions, leprosy, or corpse contamination—in the most basic terms had to do with keeping death out of the tabernacle/temple? Nothing even remotely associated with death could go near the temple, the place of God's manifest presence on the earth! This is because God is so holy that anything related to death or mortality would burn up in His presence! It was out of His great mercy, love, and grace—yes, grace is all throughout the Old Testament—that God instituted these laws as a way for people to become cleansed or purified from anything related to death so that once again they could come near His presence.

Always Drawing You Near!

You see, He *always* desires to make a way for you to draw near to Him. His heart is always for you to experience intimacy with Him, not to be distant from you. The temple is such a beautiful concrete visual of multiple attributes of God working together for good at the exact same time—grace, mercy, love, holiness, justice, righteousness, truth, and never-changing!

When the people who lived in tabernacle/temple times became ritually unclean, they had to follow quite extensive requirements to once again be ritually clean. Generally, these would include a prescribed series of water immersions and the offering of various sacrifices, depending upon the type of uncleanness. For example, when a woman gave birth to a baby boy, she became unclean for 40 days (for baby girls it was 80 days!). At various times throughout these days of being unclean, she had to fully immerse in ritual baths and then present sin offerings at the temple. When someone became contaminated by coming in contact with someone or something who had died, or even touched anything that someone else had touched who had been in contact with someone who had touched a dead body, they had to be sprinkled with a mixture of living water and the ashes of a red heifer. The requirements for selecting the red heifer and for burning the red heifer were very detailed and extensive. Interestingly enough, hyssop, scarlet yarn, and cedar wood (all symbolic of the Messiah) were also burned with the red heifer.

The Temple Reveals so Much About God!

All of this detail so clearly communicates how holy God is and how serious death is to Him. Nothing is as contaminating to God as death. Anything remotely related to mortality cannot exist in His presence without burning up! His laws were created not because He's a killjoy, but rather out of His mercy and grace to protect the people from annihilation. I love how everything about the temple communicates such powerful and healing truths to us about who God is and how much He values us!

Unbelievably, that same God—He did not change from Old Testament to New Testament, He's always the same yesterday, today and forever (see Heb. 13:8)—who instituted all these laws and commanded the people to go through all of these extensive rituals because nothing is more contaminating to Him than death—He actually *took death upon Himself* and became a corpse because He wanted *you* so badly! That's right, because He wanted *you* so badly! That's how valuable *you* are to Him!

> [Jesus,] *who, being in the form of God, did not consider it robbery to be equal with God, but made Himself of no reputation, taking the form of a bondservant, and coming in the likeness of men. And being found in appearance as a man, He humbled Himself and became obedient to the point of death, even the death of the cross* (Philippians 2:6-8).

You're So Wanted!

Even though Jesus was equal with God, He chose not to take advantage of this. How many of us love to take advantage of who we know to get good seats at a game, or a good table at a restaurant? Yet Jesus wouldn't take advantage of who He knew and who He was to get out of dying for you because He wanted you so badly; you are that valuable to Him, and He desires so intensely to be with you at all times! Now that kind of love casts out all fear!

When I dwell on this—and I do *every* morning and all throughout the day—I literally feel the fear, stress, and negativity fall off of me like a heavy blanket sliding off. I feel so wanted, so safe, so secure, so valuable, so taken care of, so loved. I can trust Him with everything and anything.

Dwelling on the temple also makes me appreciate in such a deep way what Jesus did for me when He died for me. We tend to take the cross for granted, "Oh yeah, I know Jesus died on the cross for me." However, when we study Leviticus and Numbers and understand what death really meant to Him, the fact that He would take death upon Himself and become a corpse for me and you is just insane, unfathomable, and unbelievable!

Worth That Never Changes!

When everything else is constantly changing, finding your worth, acceptance, and security in how He sees you and what He has done for you is a must. It's literally the only thing that can't change or be taken away from you! However, if you're looking to other people to love you perfectly, to others' opinions to give you worth, or to your circumstances for security, you'll never be able to stand strong against persecution, deception, or the fear and stress that comes with these constantly changing, turbulent times. When you focus on what Jesus did in order to be with you, you will grow in intimacy with Him, and you will be able to stand strong and unshaken no matter what happens!

Dwell on Him Throughout the Day: *Who He Is as He Revealed Himself*

Let's explore now how focusing throughout the day on *who He is* will increase your intimacy with God. *Who He is* may sound self-explanatory and obvious, but if we truly want to grow in intimacy with God, we need to focus on who He is as *He* has revealed Himself, not as we have defined Him to be based upon our own needs or past experiences. Let's look at some examples.

Definitions of God

Culture

Culture defines God in many different and contradictory ways. For example: as the one who sends hardship; is too weak to fix or stop evil; is so loving that He overlooks sin; is there but not involved or concerned with the details of our life; is in heaven where all people will eventually end up, but should stay out of our personal lives until then; the one we pray to when there is a natural disaster or tragedy, but is kept out of every other aspect of life, such as schools, government, media, and entertainment.

Religious Denominations

Religious denominations often present extremes of God. For example: He's all about grace and love and what *is* okay to do; He's all about fire, brimstone, and judgment and what is *not* okay to do; He's all about prosperity; He's all about hardship, suffering, and sacrifice. In other words, they are not focusing on *all* aspects of God, but are usually focusing on only one or two at the exclusion of all others.

Now, just like in any other relationship, you can't experience intimacy with someone, be it a spouse or a friend, if you are only familiar with "one side" of them or one aspect of their personality. If you only know what someone is like at work or at school, but not what they are like at home or in different settings, you can't really experience intimate relationship with them. If you only have surface knowledge of someone, but don't know the deeper matters of their heart—what drives them, what are their hopes, goals, and struggles—you can't truly experience intimacy with them. It's the same way in your relationship with Jesus. If you only know one aspect of Him—as the baby, as only love, or as only meek and mild—you can't experience intimacy with Him. The more you know about what Jesus will be like when He *comes back*—what will be on His heart, what His passions, goals, plans are for you—the more you will experience intimacy with Him *now*.

Personal Shopper

I remember when I was hired at my first "high visibility" corporate job in Long Beach, California, I went shopping at Nordstrom in the Redondo Beach Galleria to buy some corporate-looking '80s suits. Originally from Ohio, I had never been to a Nordstrom before (at that time they were still primarily located in the Seattle area), and this was my first experience ever with a personal shopper! I loved it! I told her about my job, and she did all the running around and brought everything to me. I never had to leave the dressing room for hours! I didn't even need to ask for specific items, because she knew in advance what I needed. Blouses, skirts, blazers—she mixed and matched them all for me. I had never experienced anything like this! I think many of us view God this way—that His sole purpose in our lives is to get us what we need. We don't need to ask for specifics, we just tell Him about our situation and He does all the running around for us. We don't have to do a thing besides accept or reject what He brings to us. And when He doesn't come through, we blame Him for abandoning us, being unpredictable, or paying more attention to other customers than to us!

Past Experiences

Past experiences distort how we see God. Our view of God is always filtered through our experience with authority figures and through the teachings we've heard about God. If our parents (especially Dad) were harsh, critical, impossible to please, demanded perfection, distant, etc. we will often "put their faces on God" and believe (even without being aware of it) that He sees us the same way that our earthly parents did.

However, *none* of these definitions and pictures of God are in line with how *He* has revealed Himself in His Word. Let's look at some examples.

40 Attributes of Jesus in Revelation 1–3

A great way to grow in knowledge of how He has revealed Himself in His Word is by praying through the attributes of Jesus found in Revelation chapters 1–3. The book of Revelation is all about, you guessed it, the revelation of Jesus! In the first three chapters of Revelation alone, I identified 40 attributes or characteristics of Jesus and they are:

1. Faithful witness (1:5)

2. Firstborn from the dead (1:5)

3. Ruler over the kings of the earth (1:5)

4. The one who loved us (1:5)

5. The one who washed us from our sins in His own blood (1:5)

6. The one who has made us kings and priests to God (1:6)

7. To Him belong glory and dominion forever and ever (1:6)

8. Coming with the clouds to rule all nations (1:7)

9. Every eye will see Him (1:7)

10. All the tribes of the earth will mourn because of Him (1:7)

11. Has the voice as of a trumpet (1:7)

12. Alpha (1:8)

13. Omega (1:8)

14. First (1:8)

15. Last (1:8)

16. The one who was, who is, and who is to come (1:8)

17. Stands in the midst of seven golden lampstands (1:13)

18. One like the Son of Man (1:13)

19. Clothed with the garment down to His feet (robe of the high priest) (1:13)

20. Girded about the chest with a golden band (1:13)

21. Head and hair white like wool, white as snow (1:14)

22. Eyes like flaming fire (1:14)

23. Feet like fine brass (1:15)

24. Voice like the sound of many waters (1:15)

25. Holds seven stars in His right hand (1:16)

26. A sharp, two-edged sword comes out of His mouth (1:16)

27. His countenance is like the sun shining in its strength (1:16)

28. The one who lives, was dead, and is alive forevermore (1:18)

29. Holds the keys of Hades and of death (1:18)

30. Reveals mysteries (1:20)

31. Searches minds and hearts (2:23)

32. He is Holy (3:7)

33. He is True (3:7)

34. He has the key of David (3:7)

35. He who opens and no one shuts, and shuts and no one opens. (3:7)

36. The Amen (3:14)

37. The faithful and true witness (3:14)

38. The beginning of the creation of God (3:14)

39. As many as He loves He rebukes and chastens (3:19)

40. He stands at the door, knocks, comes in and dines with anyone who hears His voice and opens the door (3:20)

How They Impact Your Daily Life

I strongly encourage you to pick one a week or even one a month to pray through every day. For example:

Eyes like Blazing Fire

"Jesus, thank You that You are the one who has eyes like blazing fire. Reveal Yourself to me in that way and show me what it means to me personally." When I prayed that prayer, Jesus impressed upon my heart that eyes like blazing fire meant that He was jealous for me when I was focused on anything or anyone else other than Him, including ministry work and my family! When I focus and dwell on anything or anyone other than Him throughout the day, He's jealous for me! That revelation of His intense desire for my attention and affection drew me into deeper intimacy with Him.

Faithful Witness

"Thank You, Jesus, that You are the faithful witness. Reveal Yourself to me as the faithful witness. Show me what it means to be a faithful witness in my own life." Be prepared for what He might reveal! Many times that week, Jesus showed me all of the often subtle ways that I was not being a faithful witness. Rather, I was more concerned about being accepted and not rejected or about avoiding conflict than I was with sharing challenging truth about Him or being honest with how I felt about something. When I became aware of the many direct and indirect ways that I am not a faithful witness, I confessed these as sin and experienced greater intimacy with Him.

Not only has praying through the attribute of "faithful witness" brought me closer to Jesus, it has also brought healing to my heart. When I was growing up, I received the message that I was not allowed to share my opinions or beliefs. Therefore, if someone (usually one of my brothers) was forcing their beliefs or opinions upon me, I had to take in whatever was coming at me. By praying through this attribute, God has brought healing to my heart by showing me that old message was a lie. He is calling me to be a faithful witness. He wants me to share what I think and believe, and to set healthy boundaries for my temple. I have a right to protect my temple! After all, if God put such elaborate systems in place to protect His earthly temples, how much more so is His heart and desire for us to protect our temples which house His Holy Spirit! It's God's desire that I stand up for what I believe, that I share the truth in love. I do have something valuable to say. I don't have to be a victim, an object, or a garbage dumpster for someone else's garbage! Therefore, praying through the attribute of "faithful witness" has convicted me, as well as brought healing salve to my heart.

The One Who Loves Us

Over the past few weeks, every day I have been praying through the attribute of "the one who loves us" (see Rev. 1:5). Again, these prayers are powerful and convicting, so be prepared to listen to what He will say! For example, the Lord showed me all the ways that I justify not being loving toward others. My husband was trying to give me his opinion on something while I was rushing, and so I snapped at him because he knew I was in a hurry; I avoid reaching out to people in social settings or I'm grumpy with family members because I'm tired, stressed out, or too busy. Once I was at a dinner where I was angry with the leader because she expected us to pay for the entire group (which wasn't fair) but that justified my lack of interest in getting to know anyone else at the table and blocked Jesus' light in me.

In general, it's easy for us to justify not having love for those who hurt us, disappoint us, treat us unfairly and push our buttons; or for those who may be against us, believe differently from us, or who we feel are responsible for the decline of this country. However, God's heart is always to have love toward others, to bless them. He spoke to me through 1 Corinthians 6:19-20 that because I am not my own, I do not have the right to choose *not* to love others! "Your body belongs to Me to show forth My heart and to accomplish My purposes." So now, when these justifications for not loving begin to creep in, I remember this verse, and I choose to be "the one who loves" as Jesus is.

> *Or do you not know that your body is the temple of the Holy Spirit who is in you, whom you have from God, and you are not your own? For you were bought at a price; therefore glorify God in your body and in your spirit, which are God's* (1 Corinthians 6:19-20).

Revelation 4 Throne Room Scene

We can also grow in intimacy by praying through each description of the throne room that is detailed in Revelation 4. "Lord, what do You want to reveal to me about *who You are* and *how You see me* from each detail of the throne room?" For example:

THRONE ROOM DESCRIPTION	WHAT IT REVEALS
He is like a jasper and sardius stone in appearance. (4:3)	Jasper—His glory radiates from Him like a diamond. He can break through any darkness. Sardius—He has fiery passion, desire, jealousy for you.

THRONE ROOM DESCRIPTION	WHAT IT REVEALS
The rainbow around the throne is like an emerald. (4:3)	He is always merciful.
24 elders' thrones surround His throne. (4:4)	He desires to rule in partnership with you, not as a driving, merciless dictator.
Lightnings, thunderings, and voices proceed from His throne. (4:5)	His Word is full of power, splendor, and truth. He desires to reveal truth to you.
Seven lamps of fire are burning. (4:5)	He is holy and powerful, yet loving to provide protection from His fiery presence.
Sea of glass like crystal before the throne. (4:6)	He is pure, perfect, and beautiful.
Living creatures (seraphim) do not rest day or night worshiping Him. (4:8)	He is worthy of your non-stop praise and worship.

Declare Scriptures

Lastly, we can focus on who He is by declaring Scriptures out loud. For example, those detailing the current throne room scene in heaven (see Rev. 4:3–11; 5:9–13; 7:10; and 15:3-4), and those which describe what He will be doing when He returns to earth (see Rev. 19:11–19; Zech. 12–14).

We exert incredible power in the heavenly realms when we declare these scriptures *out loud!* We are told in Ephesians 6:17 that the spoken word (*rhema* in the Greek) is the sword of the spirit. Therefore, every morning when I declare these passages out loud, I am using my spiritual weapon of warfare (God's Word) that cuts through the spiritual atmosphere like a sword—releasing angels and dislodging demons. I am doing warfare in the heavenly realms, changing the spiritual atmosphere around me. The enemy doesn't want us to know that we have this weapon or that we have the power to use it! He's well aware of the casualties it inflicts on his army!

Declaring these Scriptures out loud every morning also draws me into deeper intimacy with Jesus. I strongly encourage you to do the same! It gives me hope and excitement for His return. My eyes are lifted beyond what I see around me. All of my difficulties and struggles, concerns about what I have to get done, and fears about the future seem to fade away as I see myself at the side of a warrior King.

Dwell on Him Throughout the Day:
How He Sees You as His Bride

Especially in these uncertain times, it's important to focus throughout the day on how Jesus sees you as His bride, and thank Him out loud for it! When you see yourself as your bridegroom sees you, this not only keeps you strong in the midst of uncertainty, persecution, criticism, and your own failures—it also helps prepare you for who He will be when He returns as your bridegroom.

What Does Bridegroom Mean to You?

However, before you even try to focus on how Jesus sees you as His bride, first it's important to ask yourself, "Does Jesus as my bridegroom even mean anything to me; does it impact my daily life, and if not, why?" Ask Him to show you what is blocking you from seeing Him as your bridegroom and allowing His love to move your heart and impact your life. He always desires to share truth in your inmost parts!

Furthermore, this whole concept of Jesus as bridegroom might be particularly difficult for men, but hang in there with me! If He calls you *His bride* in the following Scriptures, this means you *are* able to relate to Him as your bridegroom! He will show you how, all you need to do is ask Him!

> *For I have betrothed you to one husband, that I may present you as a chaste virgin to Christ* (2 Corinthians 11:2).

> *The Spirit and the Bride say, "Come!"* (Revelation 22:17)

> *And as the bridegroom rejoices over the bride, so shall your God rejoice over you* (Isaiah 62:5).

> *At midnight there was a shout, "Behold, the bridegroom! Come out to meet him"* (Matthew 25:6 NASB).

> *Let us rejoice and be glad and give the glory to Him, for the marriage of the Lamb has come and His bride has made herself ready* (Revelation 19:7 NASB).

My Own "Bridegroom Blocker"

For me, *bridegroom* was just a term that I knew in my head, but not my heart. It never impacted my thoughts, emotions, or attitudes or made any difference in my daily life. When I asked God why this was, He revealed many reasons to me. The most significant was the conflict that existed around planning my own wedding! At 35, I had waited a long time for that day, and I wanted to invite the world! On the other hand, my bridegroom had led wedding bands all through college, playing multiple weddings every weekend! He literally hated wedding receptions and just wanted small, simple, no tacky traditions, and no band! You can only imagine our planning sessions! Now, it all worked out and we had a beautiful wedding, yet here I am, 20 years later, wondering why the concept of Jesus as my bridegroom does not have significant meaning in my life. The Lord showed me that I still harbored unforgiveness in my heart toward my husband that I was not even aware of, and that I needed to break through this in order to fully experience Jesus as my bridegroom. When I forgave and asked God to show me what Jesus as bridegroom means to me personally, He impressed upon my heart words such as:

- I delight in you.

- I can't stop rejoicing over you with singing.

- I desire you; I enjoy you.

- You're the only one for me.

- I can't take my eyes off you.

- I can't stop thinking about you.

- I miss you when you're not focused on me.

- I love being with you all the time.

- I can't wait for our wedding day.

- You bring me joy and delight.

- My heart is ravished for you!

- I'm consumed with you.

- I love 100 percent of you—even the parts you never liked or were ashamed of.

- You're beautiful to me even in your weakness.

- I'm legally committed and married to you no matter what.

- I miss you when you're sleeping.

I dwell on these truths all throughout the day, and I thank Him out loud for each one! When I see myself as His bride, my intimacy with Him soars, my needs for love are met by Him, and I know that only He can love me perfectly. Now let's put your name in those expressions of love, because Jesus is saying the same to you too!

Jesus says (insert your name), "_____*is all I can think about; I can't take my eyes off* _____. _____*brings me delight; I'm rejoicing over* _____*with singing, I love 100 percent of* _____—*even the parts that you never liked or even hated;* _____ *is the only one for me; I so enjoy being with* _____ *and I miss you when you're focused on anything other than me.* _____ *is the object of my attention and affection; I want to be with* _____*all the time!*"

The Perfect Spouse Does Exist!

Isn't that what we all want and expect from others? I believe it's God who puts the desire in our hearts for a perfect bridegroom or spouse, but only to be completely and perfectly fulfilled by Jesus Himself!

When your needs for love are met by Jesus and you acknowledge that only He can love you perfectly, it releases you from having this expectation of others and frees you to love and forgive them—just as they are—the way that God loves them. Whenever I'm having difficulty forgiving or I'm stuck in bitterness, anger, or negative emotions toward others, oftentimes it's because I've forgotten that only God can love me perfectly, only He can meet 100 percent of my needs for love, and I've been looking to a person other than Him to love me perfectly.

The Song of Solomon

Studying the Song of Solomon is another great way to learn and experience how Jesus sees you as His bride. It is packed full of expressions of His passions and emotions toward you. For example:

- You are beautiful to Him, even in your weakness. (4:7)
- You have ravished His heart—meaning filled with intense delight, enrapture, enthrall, captivate. (4:9)
- You bring Him joy and delight. (7:6,10)
- Your love is better than wine. (1:2; 4:10)
- He would rather have your love than all the works of His creation. (4:10; 6:4–10; 7:1–9)
- You are His and He is yours. (2:16; 6:3)

Thank Him throughout the Day: *Praise Him*

Because intimacy with God is the *only thing* that never changes and can't be taken away from you (unless you allow barriers to intimacy), then it only makes logical sense that you should *always* be able to experience intimacy with Him! It all depends on what you choose to focus on!

Be Thankful for What Never Changes

It will be absolutely essential as the world grows darker and more uncertain that you practice now thanking God for what you *do* know about His character, rather than focusing on what you *don't* know about your circumstances. If your eyes, hope, expectations, and stability are dependent upon your circumstances or other people, you will not be able to stand strong and be a light for Him.

View the daily struggles in your lives as practices for the future. See them as opportunities to focus on what you *do* know about God and His character, and to continually thank Him and praise Him for it. Thank Him in advance—before you ever see the evidence—for working in accordance with His Word, His will, and His character. He is more than able to call things that are not as though they were! (See Romans 4:17.)

Always Something to Thank Him For!

No matter what is going on in your world, you can always choose to thank Him for who He is, what He has done for you, how much He loves you, and how He sees you—because those things *never* change. When you do, then His love, truth, and Spirit will be controlling your mood rather than other people or your circumstances.

For example, "Thank You, Lord, that..."

- You took death upon Yourself for me—You wanted and valued me that much!
- You can't take Your eyes off me.
- You can't stop thinking about me.
- You want to be with me all the time.
- You enjoy being with me.
- I bring You delight.
- I'm beautiful to You even in my weakness.
- You love 100 percent of me.
- Your yoke is easy and Your burden is light.
- You are for me, not against me.
- You are the only one who never changes.

- You are the only one who loves me perfectly.

- You will enable me to get everything done in Your will.

- You will coordinate and orchestrate all of my interactions today.

- You will put Your will for me in their heart.

- You will carry all of my burdens for me.

- You cannot stop rejoicing over me with singing.

- You see me as perfect in the Holy of Holies.

- Your plans for me are good, to give me a future and a hope.

- You only ask only *one thing* of me!

Connect with God's Heart

The more you connect with God's heart, the more you will experience intimacy with Him. "Connecting with God's heart" means you are thinking His thoughts, feeling His emotions, speaking His words, and seeing what He sees about yourself, others, your circumstances, the nations, Jerusalem, Israel, the end times, the Millennium, and the biblical feasts. In order to do this, you first need to know what His thoughts, emotions, words, attitudes, and perspectives *are* toward all of those things. For example:

God's Heart toward You

He never condemns, accuses, criticizes, speaks condescendingly toward you, or puts you down; never puts pressure or burdens on you, gives up on you, or focuses on your weaknesses and your mistakes. Rather, He rejoices over you with singing, you bring Him great delight, He enjoys being with you, and His heart is ravished (or enthralled) for you. You are beautiful to Him even in your weakness (see Isa. 62:4-5; Zeph. 3:17; Ps. 18:19; Song of Sol. 4:7,9; Rom. 8:1; 1 Cor. 13:4–7; Col. 1:22; Eph. 1:4; Heb. 13:5; Matt. 11:30).

When you see yourself the way that God sees you, when you think and talk about yourself in the same way that He does, you connect with His heart and, by doing so, grow in intimacy with Him. However, when you put yourself down, criticize yourself, focus on your mistakes and weaknesses, or compare yourself to others ("I'm such a bad mom/dad or wife/husband, I'm so stupid, etc."), and when you make negative declarations ("I can't take one more thing, I'm not going to make it, I can't do this!"), you are not connecting with God's heart toward you. In fact, you are aligning with the enemy's thoughts toward you. Accusing, critical, negative thoughts are always from the enemy—*he* is the accuser, not God (see Rev. 12:10).

God's Heart toward Others

This same principle applies toward others. We need to see others as God does. His heart is ravished toward them, He delights in them, He forgives them, He is kind and tenderhearted toward them, He desires to bless them, He sees their potential and the purpose for which He created them, He always seeks after their good, He is not focused on their wrongs, His plans are to prosper them and not to harm them. He is always seeking to draw them near to Himself. He does not give up on them or see them as hopeless (see Col. 3:13; Eph. 4:31-32; Luke 6:28; Rom. 12:14; 1 Thess. 5:15; 1 Pet 3:9; Jer. 29:11; Ps. 25:10).

Therefore, when we are critical toward others; focus on what they are doing wrong; gossip; talk negatively about them; harbor anger, bitterness, unforgiveness, and frustration; assume the worst about them; put them down; give up on them; see them as hopeless;

or try to avoid them—we are not connecting with God's thoughts, emotions, words, and attitudes toward them. Rather, we are aligning with the enemy and giving him a handle in our lives.

When you are in agreement with God's heart (His thoughts, emotions, words, attitudes, perspectives), you increase His reign over your heart and on the earth, and you experience intimacy with Him. When you align with the enemy's thoughts, emotions, words, attitudes, and perspectives, he gets a handle (opening, influence, or foothold) in your life, you increase his reign over your heart and this world, and you cannot experience intimacy with God. It's impossible to experience deep intimacy with God when your thoughts, emotions, words, and attitudes toward yourself or others are aligning with those of the enemy.

Intimacy and Forgiveness

Let me just say a few more words about unforgiveness because it's something we all struggle with. I know I do!

It's impossible to experience deep intimacy with God and at the same time harbor unforgiveness and bitterness toward others. God's heart is always to forgive and to bless others. When you recognize that only He can love you perfectly and you connect with His heart toward that person who hurt or offended you and forgive them, you grow in intimacy with God. You also make room for God to work in the situation. On the other hand, when you choose not to forgive you remain in bondage to the other person (they're on the throne); you block God from working in you, the other person, and the situation; and you lose intimacy with God.

Now the enemy wants your eyes focused on others (instead of God) to meet your needs and to love you perfectly. When they don't, he wants you to stay focused on what they did wrong and how they hurt you. When you are stuck in unforgiveness, you align yourself with him, he gets a handle in your life, and his reign is increased in the situation.

It's so important to keep in mind that forgiveness is *not* about you and the other person! It's about re-establishing intimacy between you and God and taking back the ground in your heart that you've given to the enemy through your unforgiveness. It's a spiritual battle, not an earthly one! If you're waiting for the other person to deserve your forgiveness, it will never happen. You didn't deserve God's forgiveness, but He still forgave you!

This key principle applies to close family members as well as to those you don't even know. How often do you harbor bitterness or unforgiveness toward people you have seen in the news? Perhaps political candidates or those involved in the same-sex marriage ruling, planned parenthood operations, the refugee crisis, our indifference toward radical Islam, the treaty with Iran, or in other actions against Israel? Now, I'm not saying that those events or groups are right or that you shouldn't fight for righteousness in those situations; quite the contrary. What I am saying is that when you harbor bitterness and unforgiveness toward individuals involved in those situations, bash them with your words, and encourage others to do the same—you are giving the enemy a handle in your life and on the earth, you are blocking God from working in the situation, and you are decreasing your intimacy with God.

Intimacy in the Moment-by-Moment

Is anyone else convicted or is it just me? How many times throughout the day do you have critical or negative thoughts and words toward yourself, others, and your circumstances? For me, it's too many to count, that's for sure! Again, it's in the moment-by-moment of each day where you are either growing in intimacy with the Lord or you are aligning with the enemy and increasing his reign over your heart and this world.

Remember to be careful about rationalizing and justifying these reactions and emotions with "Wouldn't anyone react that way? Aren't these all just normal reactions? After all, we are only human!" Yes, that's true; however, we have to look behind what we can see. *"While we do not look at the things which are seen, but at the things which are not seen. For the things which are seen are temporary, but the things which are not seen are eternal"* (2 Cor. 4:18). Satan gets a handle, opening, influence, or foothold through anything in our lives that is not of God's heart.

We have to develop highly fine-tuned spiritual "antennas" that are continually on the lookout for anything in our hearts that is not in God's heart.

It's staying in intimacy with God in these moment-by-moment choices that will enable you to stand strong in these uncertain times. If you can't experience intimacy with God *now* in the moment-by-moment, how will you ever be able to when life as you know it is crashing in all around you? If the economy collapses, if terrorism occurs within our borders, if our world becomes increasingly unsafe, or if you are persecuted for your faith? Intimacy has to start *now* in the moment-by-moment places. It's not something you can receive by attending a seminar or a class and getting a "Certificate in Intimacy with God." I'm convinced that God gives you millions of opportunities each day to practice so that you will grow stronger *now* in intimacy with Him and then be able to stand firm when times become even more uncertain or more turbulent. You may not be able to stop ISIS and what's going on in Syria or be able to predict the start of the tribulation or when Jesus is coming back, but you *can* deal with anything that blocks intimacy with God.

So what do you do when you find that you've aligned your-self with the enemy? When you don't have God's heart toward yourself, others, your circumstances, the nations, Israel, the future? That is the focus of the next chapter—how to use spiritual weapons of warfare to break free from these barriers and experience even greater intimacy with God as a result! Remember what the enemy intends for evil and to bring death and destruction, God will use for good!

Chapter 4

Intimacy Blockers

Looking once again to the football game analogy, to experience ongoing intimacy with God, in addition to taking the *offensive* steps detailed in Chapter 3, you must also have *defensive* strategies in place. That means being aware of and committed to dealing with anything and everything that blocks intimacy with God!

Most of us go throughout our day reacting to people and circumstances, all the while completely unaware of how our moment-by-moment thoughts, emotions, words, and attitudes block our intimacy with God. If we ever do stop long enough to think about barriers to intimacy with God, we tend to focus on "the big things" rather than the subtle, moment-by-moment things.

For example, we are aware that "the big things" block our intimacy with God, such as: adultery, homosexuality, fornication, sexual promiscuity, murder, theft, abortion, lying, etc. And yes, I would agree that those "big sins," mess-ups, and failures in our lives can definitely destroy our intimacy with God.

However, it is absolutely critical that you also recognize the significant impact that your moment by moment thoughts, emotions, attitudes and words have on your depth of intimacy with God. It's in the moment-by-moment where you have the most opportunity to either grow closer in intimacy with God and increase His reign in your life or distance yourself from Him and increase the enemy's reign in your life.

Not only are most of us unaware of how the moment-by-moment things block our intimacy with God, we are also unaware that they are sin. It's easier for us to see the "big things" as sin and excuse the moment-by-moment fear, stress, frustration, negativity, anger, drivenness, etc., with:

- "Anyone would feel that way."

- "Who wouldn't be afraid?"

- "They hurt me, it's their fault, they are in the wrong."

- "Everyone is stressed! That's just a normal, expected way of life these days."

- "That's just my personality; that's just the way I am."

- "Performing with utmost excellence, being responsible for everything, Christian righteous anger, etc. are all good things! God expects these of me!"

- "The Bible never says, 'Do not stress!'"

Let's look at a list of typical, daily, moment-by-moment blockers to intimacy with God. As you read over this list, I'd like you to mark whether a) you see this as *sin* that blocks your intimacy with God, or b) you see this as a *normal part of everyday life* and that anyone would feel that way.

Intimacy Blockers: Sin or Normal Life?

Sin	Normal Life	
		Stressed from:
☐	☐	How behind you are and the fear that you won't get it all done
☐	☐	Feeling overwhelmed with all that lies ahead
☐	☐	Running late
☐	☐	The demands of work, home, and administration such as taxes, bills, insurance claims
☐	☐	The demands of ministry, serving others
☐	☐	Being responsible for everything/everyone—trying to hold all things/relationships together
☐	☐	Wanting to make sure everything is perfect (an event, you, your family, house, work, grades, ministry)
☐	☐	Multi-tasking, being "ultra-productive"
☐	☐	Health issues (self, family, friends)
☐	☐	Financial concerns
☐	☐	Problems with children, teens, adult children
☐	☐	Watching the news, fearing "What's next? what is coming to this country?"
☐	☐	Watching the news, fearing all the violence, terrorism, natural disasters, financial collapse, moral decline, loss of freedoms, Islamic invasion, etc.
☐	☐	Fear of end-times posts/videos on social media
☐	☐	Fear of end-times predictions
☐	☐	Relationship conflicts and struggles—family, work, friends
☐	☐	Not being liked or accepted; others' disapproval or criticism
☐	☐	Taking in others' stress, fears, anger, problems

Sin	Normal Life	
		Stressed from:
☐	☐	Receiving an unexpected email, text, or phone call that is accusing, demanding, negative, bad news, etc.

Sin	Normal Life	
		Frustrated from:
☐	☐	Trying to order from a website that won't work properly
☐	☐	Being on hold for an extended time
☐	☐	Getting stuck in an endless loop of voicemail prompts with no "live" person (a favorite stressor of mine)
☐	☐	A telephone customer service rep who is very slow at handling an issue
☐	☐	Getting the runaround from an insurance company
☐	☐	A professional who is running late or wasting time after you rushed to get there
☐	☐	Continual distractions when you're trying to get something done
☐	☐	Someone who is dominating a discussion
☐	☐	Heavy traffic; someone driving slowly in front of you when you're in a hurry
☐	☐	Not being able to find something you've lost

Sin	Normal Life	
		Angry toward:
☐	☐	Someone "pushing your buttons"—a remark, look, a tone of voice that is critical, accusatory, or condescending

Sin	Normal Life	
☐	☐	**_Angry toward:_**

Angry toward:

Sin	Normal Life	
☐	☐	Someone being inconsiderate, selfish, mistreating you or family member
☐	☐	Someone (or God) having too many/too high of expectations of you
☐	☐	Someone continually telling you what you're doing wrong, what needs to be done
☐	☐	Someone who said something offensive to you (intentional or not)
☐	☐	Someone in the news or social media

Sin Normal Life

Critical toward others:

Sin	Normal Life	
☐	☐	Having negative or critical thoughts/words about others, for example: "They talk so much, they're selfish, controlling, stuck up, spoiled, annoying, fake, manipulative, a hypocrite, hopeless, they're ruining everything, it's all their fault."
☐	☐	Focusing on and/or making lists of what they do wrong, how they've hurt you, their weaknesses and shortcomings, not recognizing their potential, and not seeing them as someone God's heart is ravished for
☐	☐	Assuming the worst about others' intentions and motives
☐	☐	Being envious of what they have/what they posted on social media—"Must be nice that they have money to do that, they're always going somewhere, can't believe they let their kids do that, they are such braggers, look at their makeup, clothes, spouse, friends," etc.

Sin	Normal Life	
		Critical toward others:
☐	☐	Sharing negative views toward others with spouse or other family members ("It doesn't count as gossip, does it, if we keep it in the family?")
☐	☐	"Christian righteousness anger" toward someone with opposing views (There's a big difference between anger toward the issue and anger toward the person.)
☐	☐	"Bashing" government leaders, election candidates
☐	☐	"Bashing" those with opposing views on social media posts

Sin	Normal Life	
		Critical toward yourself:
☐	☐	Being critical of yourself—seeing yourself as bad, inadequate, inferior, not good enough, deserving rejection, comparing yourself to others. "They're so much more _____ than I am." Believing the messages of the world about your worth—that it's based on what you do, your appearance, what you have, who you know

Sin	Normal Life	
		Dread/Negativity/Hopelessness:
☐	☐	Focusing on the negative in people and situations
☐	☐	Negative, hopeless thoughts and words about your or others' circumstances: "I'm not going to make it. I can't keep up. I'm going to fail. I'm overwhelmed. I can't carry these burdens. This is too much for me. They/things will never get better. There's no hope of change for this person/situation. It will always be this

Sin	Normal Life	
		Dread/Negativity/Hopelessness: way! They're hopeless, lost. I'm never going to get everything done! I'm never going to get out from under this mess! I'm so behind. God won't answer my prayers."
☐	☐	Choosing to hold on to negative emotions such as fear, stress, unforgiveness, anger, resentment, bitterness, blame, shame, rejection, performance, self-condemnation, critical attitudes, frustration, dread, hopelessness, negativity, etc. because they are justified.

Sin or Normal Part of Life?

Now I'm curious, as you read through the above list—how many did you mark as being sin and how many did you mark as being just a normal part of life? Well, the truth is they are *all* sin! "What?" You may be shouting at me now, "You're legalistic!" Maybe so, but I'd prefer to consider myself as "realistic." I want to know the truth, the reality about whether or not something is sin in my life. Why? Because sin gives Satan a handle (opening, influence, foothold) and it blocks my intimacy with God. If I'm committed to dealing with anything that blocks my intimacy with God, then I want to know whether or not something is sin so that I know how to deal with it!

The Right Tools for the Job

If it's properly diagnosed as sin, then the good news is I already have the tools I need to be free of it—my *spiritual* weapons of warfare! When I teach, I often use a tool belt as a visual prop to represent our spiritual weapons of warfare. As believers, God gives each one of us a "tool belt" to wear every day, chock-full of spiritual weapons of warfare. These spiritual weapons of warfare are powerful and mighty (see 2 Cor. 10:4)—they literally cut through our spiritual atmospheres, releasing angels and dislodging demons.

Using Spiritual Weapons of Warfare

Do you want to see change in your life and the lives of others? Do you want to be free from fear, stress, and everything that blocks intimacy with God? Do you want to stand strong and unshaken in uncertain times? Start using *spiritual* weapons of warfare instead of earthly weapons such as worrying, talking about it, denying it, blaming others, complaining, lashing out, trying to control, manipulate, or fix the person or the situation.

The problem is, too few of us ever take our spiritual weapons out of our tool belts and use them. Satan tries his best to keep us ignorant to the fact they are there and how to use them. Most of the time, we are not even aware that we need them because we have bought into the world's lie that these "little" moment-by-moment thoughts, emotions, words, and attitudes are not sin! Therefore, we remain in bondage to them and don't experience abundant life and freedom in the midst of uncertainty. Instead, we end up blaming God for being distant, unpredictable, and for not being able to feel His presence!

Breaking Through the Fear Blocker

Let's take a look at how we can use our spiritual weapons of warfare to break through fear of end-times predictions from the list of *intimacy blockers*. Remember my "Paralyzed by Fear" story back in the first chapter? I was paralyzed with fear that night after hearing about all of the terrible things that were going to happen to this nation and to my own family. Now, I could have easily said,

"Anyone would be fearful after hearing that news," and then spent the rest of my days hiding out, waiting for Jesus' return, being fearful and stressed just like everyone else. That's exactly what the enemy would have wanted—I make no progress increasing Jesus' kingdom on this earth, I look no different from anyone else who doesn't know Jesus, I block God's light and His purposes through me for these times, and I don't experience intimacy with God. That's *always* the enemy's agenda—*he comes to steal, kill, and destroy!* (See John 10:10.)

However, especially when you find yourself in those situations where fear seems like the natural thing to do, it is critical you remember that fear is not from God. "For God has **not** given us a spirit of fear, but of power and of love and of a sound mind" (2 Tim 1:7).

For example, in this situation I was believing the following lies:

Lies About God

- God disappeared; He abandoned me.

- Because these are the end times, He has no more involvement in my life until the rapture. Until then, He's going to stand back, watch it all happen, and allow evil to reign.

- He is no longer with me or protecting me; He is basically non-existent.

- He's pulling out of the battle; I'm left in it *by* myself to fight *for* myself.

- He is out of the picture of my life.

- He's inaccessible (until Jesus comes back).

Lies About Myself

- I'm unprotected.

- I'm all alone.

- I have to fight for myself.

- I'm not going to make it.

- I'm on my own now.

- I'm totally abandoned.

- I have no hope; there is nothing I can do to make a difference.

- I can't question messages from authority. I have to take what is spoken to me.

Below are other lies that we often believe when we fear:

Lies About God

- He's not there.

- He's not with me.

- He's unpredictable. Sometimes He's with me, sometimes He's not.

- He's with me when I'm perfect, but not when I mess up.

- He's abandoned me.

- He "tricked" me—lead me down the wrong path to a closed door.

- He wants me to learn the hard way.

- He's distant.

- He's just watching - waiting for me to "figure it out" or "get it together"

- He's not able to help.
- He's not interested in these details of my life. He's got more important things to focus on.
- He can't or won't help/be with me in this area.
- He's only involved in "spiritual things."
- He's demanding.
- He's critical.
- He's on "their side."
- He won't help me because it's my fault.
- He's expecting me to carry the burdens.
- He's mad/disappointed in me.
- He can't meet all of my needs.
- He can't/won't protect me.

Lies About Myself

- I'm all alone, I'm on my own.
- I have to be strong, I can't be weak.
- I have to hold all things/all people together.
- I have to carry the burdens.
- I'm responsible for everything.
- It's up to me to fix.
- I must be able to multitask.
- I must be able to keep up with everyone's expectations of me.
- I have to be perfect.
- I'm bad.

- I'm to blame. It's all my fault.

- I've done it this time.

- I can't protect myself/I'm unprotected.

- I have to "take in" their anxiety/their anger.

- I can't say no.

- I can't hear God's voice.

- I'm not perfect enough to be used by God.

- I can't live without _____.

- I can't be happy without _____.

- I need _____ to meet my needs.

- I need _____ to feel secure.

- I need _____ to feel loved.

- I need _____ to be happy.

- If _____ is taken away, I won't survive.

- If I stand for truth and face rejection/disapproval, then _____.

Where's God in the Picture?

Often you are not even aware that you're believing these lies that are hidden deep in your heart, and you need to ask God to reveal them to you. If someone were to come up to you and ask if you believed that God was out of the picture, you would probably say, "*No*, of course not, He would never leave me or forsake me." However, we're not talking about head knowledge here. If you really believed deep down in your heart that He was with you, would you ever experience fear? *No!* Therefore, whenever you do fear, it's also always important to ask God to show you, "Where are You, God, in the picture?" or, "Where have I put You in the picture, God?"

Whenever I ask that question, the answer is always, "God's not in the picture!" or perhaps He's there, but He's just watching. Maybe He's expecting me to carry the burdens (because the burdens are from Him), or He's expecting me to figure it out. It's also very important to ask God to reveal whether you are putting someone else's face on God—your mother, father, or other authority figure, even a spouse. Perhaps you believe in your heart that because they saw you a certain way or they interacted with you in a certain way, that God is doing the same. For example, God expects you to be perfect, or He sees you as a failure, He's not always there for you, He thinks you are bad, He's disappointed in you—just like they were.

Whenever you are believing these lies about God and about yourself in your heart, you are actually aligning yourself with the enemy and giving him reign over those areas of your heart. You have more power than you think you do! You have power to either increase Jesus' reign over your heart or increase the enemy's reign over your heart!

Seeing the Lies as Sin

When you are in agreement with what God says, His voice, you increase His reign over your heart and release His power in your life. When you are in agreement with lies and with what the enemy says, because he is the father of lies (see John 8:44) you increase his reign over your heart and release his power in your life. When you align yourself with lies from the father of lies, that is sin. Romans 14:23 tells us that *everything that does not come from faith is sin.*

It is *crucial* that you recognize the spiritual battle behind fear and stress or else you will be deceived into thinking that it's justified, anyone would feel that way, it's a part of the culture, it's just the way you are, your personality, etc. If you are committed to intimacy with God, and you truly believe it is your number-one anchor for standing strong in these uncertain times, then you must be committed to dealing with fear and stress as *sin!*

The reason we have such difficulty breaking free from bondage in our lives is because our culture and many churches have desensitized us to sin. Instead of calling sin for what it is, we call it an "issue" or a normal part of life. The sad news is because we don't call it sin, we have no hope of being freed from it!

So, back to the story, what were the spiritual weapons of warfare that I used to break through my paralyzing fear of the end times?

They are actually very simple. The older I get with the Lord, the more I realize His ways are clear and simple. They are not complicated; they are not confusing. You don't have to be a Bible scholar to figure out how to be free from fear and stress. He has made the way for *all* to come to Him and experience intimacy with Him, so whenever we think it's just too hard or too confusing, even in that we are believing a lie of the enemy!

Here they are in a nutshell.

Spiritual Weapons of Warfare

- Confess the lie/emotion as *sin* (see Rom. 14:23; 1 John 1:9; 2 Cor. 7:1; Heb. 11:6, 12:1).

- Forgive those who have wronged you (see Col. 3:13; Eph. 4:31-32; Matt. 18:34-35).

- Cancel Satan's authority (see Eph. 4:27; James 4:7; 1 John 3:8; Luke 9:1: Matt. 28:18).

- Ask the Lord to speak His truth to your heart (see Ps. 107:20; Eph. 1:18-19, 3:17–19).

Spiritual Weapons of Warfare for Fear of End Times

1. I confessed my fear and the lies that I was believing as sin.

2. I forgave anyone who had hurt me—the man who declared all of these horrific things onto my family and nation, my friends who introduced me to him, and my family who fired the original arrows at my heart that were filled with the enemy's lies.

3. I commanded the spirits of fear, rejection, and abandonment to go in the name of Jesus.

4. I cancelled the authority I had given the enemy by agreeing with his thoughts and lies that were telling me I'm unprotected, God's abandoned me, etc. (I did this for each specific lie I was believing).

5. I asked God to heal my heart and show me His truth about this situation.

So often we complain that God is not there, He won't speak to us, or that He speaks to everyone else (the more spiritual ones) but not to us! Actually, we experience this because we are hanging on to ropes (picture yourself holding on to one end of the rope and the enemy holding on to the other) that block God from speaking to us! It's only when we use spiritual weapons of warfare to cut the ropes that we are free to hear from God in a very personal way that speaks truth and healing to our hearts.

Once I cut the ropes (steps 1–4 above), God spoke *His* truth to my heart about the situation (step 5):

- Focus on what you *do* know, not on what you *don't* know. Focus on what you *do* know about God and how He is guiding and moving in your life now, not on what you *don't* know will happen.

- I was putting my dad and brothers' faces on God. God does not shut me out or stay behind an impenetrable wall. He loves being with me and delights in me.

- What we do now *does* matter in the future. It is never His will for us to give up and hide out until He returns. He reminded me of the Parable of the Talents and what happened to the servant who gave up and did nothing until the Master returned. It is always worthwhile to move forward to increase His reign and to increase righteousness that will continue on through the Millennium.

- Intercessory prayer can change the course of world events. All of the predictions are not a done deal. Pray for repentance and revival, to bind the spirit of deception, and for hearts to be open to receive truth.

- He wants us to partner with Him *now* to release His end-times plans and purposes. He has called us to action and purpose for such a time as this—not to hide out in fear.

These truths healed my heart of fear and inspired me to write this book! What a perfect example of how Satan's schemes always bring death—to our bodies, emotions, and relationships—and hinder forward movement, whereas God's voice always brings life and forward motion!

The Stress Blocker

Next, let's take a look at how *stress* is sin and blocks our intimacy with God. "What's wrong with stress? Isn't everyone *supposed* to be stressed? Isn't that an expected, normal part of life these days? Scripture tells us that fear is not from God, but it never mentions stress!" Well, maybe so, but in my opinion stress is just the socially acceptable word for fear. It's the new norm in our culture—both inside and outside of the church! In fact, if you're not stressed, that must mean you're not doing enough, you're lazy, a loser, not keeping up, not in tune with all of the latest technology, social media groups, etc. Fitting in these days includes being stressed out!

However, regardless of whether or not it's justified, you must be aware that Satan gets a handle through your stress! He just wants an open window or door to sneak in to block God's purposes in your life. He doesn't care how He gets in, He just wants in! He loves it when you don't see stress as sin, because then you won't use spiritual weapons of warfare to break free from it. You'll remain in bondage—not experiencing intimacy with God and being ineffective in accomplishing His purposes for this time. This is exactly where the enemy wants you. Yes, even stress is a tool of the enemy used in the spiritual battle that rages against you 24/7. As I mentioned before, it's time to open your eyes to the spiritual battle or else you will never stand strong in these end times!

Let me tell you from experience, it's impossible to be stressed and experience intimacy with God. Now, I'm not talking about eternal salvation or having a relationship with God—of course stress does not change that. I'm talking about experiencing *intimacy* with Him, being in His presence which results in goodness, peace, and joy—all the fruits of the spirit!

> *But the fruit of the spirit is love, joy, peace, patience, kindness, goodness, faithfulness, gentleness, self-control; against such things there is no law* (Galatians 5:22-23 NASB).

I can write with authority on this topic of stress because it's an area where God is continually showing me my need to use spiritual weapons of warfare! For example, just yesterday I felt so stressed because of all the burdens I was carrying. Worried that I wasn't going to be able to finish this book in time, feeling hopeless that I would ever catch up on the mountains of administrative work that I'm behind in, tired of continually praying for a miracle in my husband's work situation, grieved at the pain that my daughter was experiencing at school, frustrated that I wasn't making any progress toward the things that need to be done to move the ministry forward and expand His message, unsure of how we were going to manage financially. I felt completely drained, exhausted, and stressed. Have you ever experienced this? In my head I knew I shouldn't feel that way, I knew God was there, but I felt so overwhelmed I couldn't take one more thing. I just wanted to go back to bed and hide. All the things I was behind in and that needed to get done seemed to shout out at me in a condemning tone everywhere I looked in my own house. The checkbooks hadn't been balanced in months, QuickBooks entries had not been made all year, insurance claims had not been submitted all year, expense reports were a year behind, just to name a few in the administrative area!

I'd been working on this chapter for weeks and it just wasn't coming together. I still had many more chapters to write and less than a month to complete them.

All of these reasons seemed to justify my stress; anyone would feel the same stress in this situation—the circumstances justified it! However, I knew that the stress was giving Satan a handle in my life. I did not feel God's presence, I didn't have His love for others and I certainly didn't have His joy. I could just picture the rope that was connecting me to the enemy through this stress.

Spiritual Weapons of Warfare for Stress

I knew that I had to use my spiritual weapons of warfare, and so this is what I did:

1. I confessed the stress and negativity as sin.

2. In the name of Jesus, I commanded the spirits of fear, false burden bearing, anger, and bitterness to go.

3. I cancelled the authority I had given the enemy by agreeing with his thoughts and lies that were telling me:

   - I wasn't going to make it;
   - It was too much for me;
   - God wasn't there to help me with all the details (just the big picture);
   - God put all of these expectations on me that were impossible for me to meet;
   - Somehow my job was to carry all of these burdens;
   - I had to get it all done in my own strength, on my own, by myself;
   - It was just impossible to do it all.

4. I asked God to heal my heart and show me His truth about this situation. He reminded me:

- I wasn't giving all of my burdens over to Him to carry; I was believing the lie that He wanted me to carry them all.

- His yoke is easy and His burden is light. Whenever I am feeling that my burden is too much it means I'm carrying burdens that aren't mine to carry.

- I had lost my one thing focus of intimacy with Him—that's what He wants from me, not for me to work for Him or carry all of these burdens!

- I was not bringing Him into every situation. I wasn't asking for His help and thanking Him in advance for enabling me to get every single detail done.

I chose to give all of these burdens to Him to carry and thanked Him out loud that His yoke is easy and His burden is light. The next time something came to mind that I had to get done or I saw something in the house that reminded me of what I am behind in, instead of allowing the negative, hopeless, overwhelming thoughts and emotions to settle in I praised Him and thanked Him out loud that in His timing and in His will He will enable me to get it done, and that He cares and wants to be involved with every single detail of my life. Truly, I am *never* alone! I felt His peace and presence again and recommitted myself to deal with anything that blocks intimacy with Him. Even though the stress may have been justified, it's just not worth giving the enemy a handle in my life and losing intimacy with Him!

So far, I've focused on fear and stress as examples of intimacy blockers. There are many more, too many to cover in this book!

Regardless of whether the barriers are related to anger, bitterness, resentment, shame, unforgiveness, rejection, blame, performance, or self-condemnation, they all need to be and can be broken by using *spiritual* weapons of warfare!

Strongholds

Sometimes when we react in the ways that I've listed under "Intimacy Blockers" above, we are acting out of what I refer to as *strongholds*. These are lies we believe about ourselves and about God that end up driving and directing what we think, feel, say, and how we react. A sure sign of a stronghold is when we overreact to someone "pushing our button" or when we just "can't get over it" when someone offends us or something unexpected happens. They are rooted in old messages that we took into our hearts, usually when we were very young, although it can happen at any time throughout our lives. These messages may come from our parents, siblings, spouses, authority figures such as coaches and teachers, or from our culture and media.

I'd like to share a few of my own personal examples of strongholds to illustrate both how they can block intimacy as well as how powerfully and lovingly God can heal them. Without a doubt, His heart is to heal my heart and yours!

Stronghold Example #1: "The Fountain of Youth"

Throughout my entire adult life, whenever someone would say I looked young for my age or guess my age incorrectly (which 100 percent of people do) or address me as "Honey" or "Sweetie," I would completely shut down and want to avoid that person. I know it sounds extreme (reactions to strongholds often are), but I would feel worthless, inadequate, incompetent, not real, not valid, not credible, and stupid! It was as if everything I'd ever done or accomplished was erased and deemed meaningless. I would instantly be transported back to the old, worthless position of being the youngest in my family, and it would debilitate me for days! Now, my guess is that most of you would love to be perceived as looking younger than you actually are! Especially these days, when there is such an emphasis on looking "forever young." That is why I use this example because it so clearly illustrates that when you're acting out of a stronghold, it is not something that you can reason your way out of feeling. Often others can't understand your reaction and tell you to "just get over it," but you can't!

When I would shut down in those circumstances, the old messages about myself were controlling me rather than how God sees me. Again, this is sin because I'm believing lies about myself rather than God's truth about myself. Satan is the father of lies; therefore, they are not of faith and Romans 14:23 tells us that whatever is not of faith is sin. I hope you can see that this is not just a matter of my personality, my sensitivities, or my dysfunctional family— this is serious warfare, and so I needed to fight back with *spiritual* weapons of warfare!

This particular example might sound trivial and silly to you, but it was deeply painful for me and it would debilitate me for days! Now, of course Satan knew this, and so all he had to do to knock me out of the game for a while was just have someone make a comment about my age. It worked every time! He knows just what will push my buttons, and he knows what will push yours! He's not very creative, so he'll use the same buttons over and over as long as they're working and as long as we're not seeing our reactions to and agreement with the lies as sin.

"I love 100 percent of you!"

When I started using my spiritual weapons of warfare every time I received a "you look so young" comment, then healing began to take place. One of the very personal truths that God spoke to my heart about this was "I love 100 percent of you," meaning even the things about myself that I have always hated. I always hated that I looked young, and below that reaction was the hatred of that little girl who was considered so worthless. You see, the *symptom* of not liking that I look young for my age is not the real issue; it's pain from the messages I received that is the root of the symptom. Being the youngest brought messages that I was worthless, not valid, not real, useless, not valuable, not productive, a waste, incompetent, and inadequate. As a child, I took those messages in as truth and hated that "young" part of myself. When God spoke to my heart His healing words, "I love 100 percent of you," He was telling me that He loved even that part of me that felt worthless as a child. He told me that He was there with me when I was a little girl, loving me all the time, I just didn't know that He was there. The enemy deceived me even as a child into believing that I was all alone. These stronghold messages are usually formed at a very young age; in fact, sometimes even in the womb! The enemy begins working to steal, kill, and destroy from the moment of conception!

Now, every time I receive a "young" comment, I smile because I'm reminded that God loves even that young part of me that I always viewed as worthless and useless. It's taken me many years to experience complete healing, and I still feel a bit of a twinge when it happens, but it no longer affects me and robs me of life. Not because I push it down, try not to think about it, or deny that it bothers me, but because I have allowed God to heal my heart of the strongholds that were at the root of my reactions.

Stronghold Example #2: "The Strong Personality"

Last week, I received a call from someone who has a very strong personality and who was trying to pressure me into something that I didn't agree with. I very clearly let her know my thoughts on the situation, but then I just couldn't let go of the tidal waves of emotions that were overtaking me—feelings of anger, hurt, bitterness, resentment, fear, dread, and hopelessness. These feelings continued to control me the rest of the day even though I kept trying *not* to let them do this. When we are controlled by our strongholds, it comes out in other areas as well. For example, I became less patient with my daughter and husband, snapped at them more easily, got hurt by something they said, and was overly sensitive in general. Strongholds cause an emotional and spiritual cancer (and oftentimes physical as well) that spreads to every area of your life.

When I confessed these feelings as sin and asked God to show me what lies I was believing, He showed me that I was believing:

- She was going to push me over my limit, way beyond what I could handle, as well as thrust me back into my old identity in the family of being a dumpster for everyone else's problems.

- God was powerless compared to her; either He could do nothing about it or He wanted me to do this, and somehow I was bad if I was not able to do it all!

Do you see the lies (fueled by the father of lies) that were driving the thoughts, emotions, attitudes, behaviors? Where was God in that picture? He was powerless, and He wanted this pressure for me! Behind fear, stress, and all the negative emotions, there are *always* lies that we are believing about ourselves and about God!

When I used my weapons of warfare, I confessed all the negative emotions; I chose to forgive this person for trying to take over; I commanded the spirits of fear, bitterness, and abandonment to go; and I cancelled the power and authority I'd given to Satan by believing each of the lies I described above (this cuts the ropes to the enemy). Then God showed me the following truths that brought instant healing to my heart.

"He's Married to Me!"

He brought to mind a picture of a wedding ring on my finger. He reminded me that He's married to me. He's legally committed to me, it's a legal transaction or agreement. He can't break it, He can't stop defending me. No one (even this powerful person) can snatch me out of His hands! He's my legal bridegroom, I belong to Him, and He has authority over me—no one else! He is my defense! He is on the throne and all powerful, He is not powerless in comparison to this person, He is above all and is the name that is above *all names!*

When God spoke His words to my heart and showed me the picture of our ring, it drew me into such intimacy with Him. I felt loved, protected, special, taken care of, and not at all alone and abandoned. That's the kind of intimacy we need to stay strong and unshaken in uncertain times! His words filled the stronghold holes in my heart and brought healing. All of the fear, shame, bitterness, anger, resentment, etc. fell away in a moment! I haven't thought about it since, whereas before I used my spiritual weapons of warfare I could think of nothing else!

Can you see how Satan wants to rob you of life through these strongholds? They keep your mind, thoughts, emotions, and words focused on everything else but God, and yet it's only in Him that we have perfect peace and in His presence is fullness of joy!

You will keep him in perfect peace, whose mind is stayed on You (Isaiah 26:3).

In Your presence is fullness of joy (Psalms 16:11).

Stronghold Example #3: "He Chooses Not to Help Her!"

My daughter was going through a very difficult time at school academically and socially and was experiencing intense stress. Of course as her mother I was very concerned for her physically, emotionally, and spiritually. One night when she was feeling extremely down, I encouraged her to go to her horse lesson because that always brings her joy and boosts her confidence. Well, that night she ended up falling off of her horse and hit the ground hard. Now I know from previous falls this means endless hours at various doctors, physical therapists, and chiropractor appointments. I went into fear and dread mode! If she has to go to all of these appointments, how will she ever keep up with these school assignments that are already overwhelming her? How will I be able to take her to them? We had company coming in that weekend and now she won't be able to enjoy it; she'll be in pain and all we'd planned for the past year will be ruined!

I felt completely defeated and that God was nowhere to be found. He was silent and not answering my prayers. You see, I had been praying nonstop for a breakthrough in her difficult situations, and instead of God bringing her relief in *any* way, she fell. I spiraled down into the pit of negativity, hopelessness, and dread—now everything is ruined for her, she just can't get a break, she's not going to make it, this is the final icing for her, the straw that broke the camel's back, there's no hope in this situation, God just won't listen to my prayers for her.

When I prayed and asked God to show me what lie I was believing, he showed me that I believed God is there for me, He is always with me, working for my good, desiring to bless me, never abandons me, and answers my prayers—however, He refuses to be there and do the same for Charis. It's not that He's powerless as in my last example; He has the power, yet He *chooses* not to use it in this case, He chooses *not* to help Charis for some reason.

You see these lies were rooted way back starting in my earliest moments with Charis after her birth. Now we understand her regulatory issues, but at the time there was no explanation as to why she was unable to sleep. As a newborn infant, she literally could not sleep for more than 1 hour in a 24-hour period, and all throughout the remaining 23 hours she was in a state of constant distress! I would *beg* God to make her fall asleep; after all, He is all-powerful and can do anything—surely He could make her fall asleep, but He didn't! So when she fell off her horse that night, all of those old lies about God from her infancy that had never been healed came back in full force!

Out of the Darkness

When these lies are brought out into the light, it's actually a good thing because then and only then can they be healed! When they stay hidden in your heart, they can never be healed, and their only use is to give Satan a handle in your life. God doesn't cause these things to come up, but when situations trigger them He uses them for good to show you where you are giving the enemy a handle in your life and what still needs to be healed. Remember, His number-one desire for you is intimacy with Him, and so He *desires* to reveal anything that blocks intimacy if you will just allow Him to!

Even when we think we are completely healed of a stronghold, the intensity of our reactions when our buttons get pushed or our inability to let go of our negative emotions tells us that we are not and that there are still areas God needs and wants to heal.

Drawing Us Near

When I used my weapons of warfare and asked God to show me His truth about the situation, a few days later (He doesn't always speak immediately, but in His perfect timing) He brought the following scriptures to mind from a sermon I had listened to earlier that week while I was cleaning the kitchen and didn't even realize had penetrated (truly His word does not return void):

> *Of a truth I perceive that God is no respecter of persons* (Acts 10:34 KJV).
>
> *For there is no respect of persons with God* (Romans 2:11 KJV).

He is no respecter of persons! He doesn't withhold His love and His purposes for just a select few and ignore or refuse to bless the rest (who are seeking Him). I thought about all of the evidence we have in His Word that proves He desires intimacy with us and always makes a way for us to draw near to Him. I was reminded of the temple and how everything about the temple services—the sacrifices and laws of ritual purity—was designed to make a way for sinful man to draw near to Him. Jesus came to this earth in the form of a man to die for us—again, God's perfect plan and design of making a way for us to draw near to Him.

God's intense desire to draw near to us, and for us to draw near to Him, is not only for a select few; rather, this is His heart for *everyone*! It is His desire that none should perish (see 2 Pet. 3:9). It is His heart that all would draw near to Him and experience intimacy with Him. He shows no partiality. That truth penetrated and filled the hole in my heart and brought healing to the lie that He desired to help everyone but Charis. It brought healing in today's situation; it also brought healing to those unhealed wounds from 14 years ago.

God is *so* faithful to heal our hearts when we do our part to use our weapons of warfare! By cutting the ropes and handles that we've given to the enemy, we allow Him to penetrate and speak to our hearts in a very personal way that will be special and meaningful uniquely to us. Only *He* understands the original wounds of our strongholds, and only *He* knows *exactly* what will heal our hearts!

When our hearts experience healing from these strongholds, the enemy loses ground and Jesus' reign increases—both in our hearts and in this world. We experience deeper intimacy with God, and as a result we are able to stand strong and unshaken no matter what the circumstances because we are controlled by His Spirit and His Word, not by our strongholds!

Intimacy Checks

Here are a few helpful questions I'd encourage you to ask yourself throughout the day as "check-ups" on how you're doing in terms of intimacy with the Lord.

1. *What's determining my mood right now?*

A great barometer for gaging your level of intimacy with God throughout the day is to ask yourself, "What's determining my mood right now? What's determining whether I feel joy or frustration and negativity? hope or dread? love or criticism toward others and myself? peace and God's presence or fear and stress?"

God recently showed me that if my mood is characterized by anything other than the fruit of the spirit—love, joy, peace, patience, kindness, goodness, faithfulness, gentleness, self-control (see Gal. 5:22)—then I've stopped focusing on that *one thing*. More than likely I'm focused on multiple things, and I've put someone or something other than Him on the throne of my life at that moment! I'm worshiping whoever or whatever is controlling my mood instead of God.

For me, it could be my husband, my daughter, siblings, in-laws, government leaders, customer service reps, frustration with being so behind in all that needs to get done, distractions, feeling overwhelmed with ministry projects, a comment someone has made, a text, an email, frustration with taxes, fear and negativity from watching the news, and the list goes on.

When you find that you are not displaying the fruits of the Spirit because something or someone (other than intimacy with God) is determining your mood, it's important right then to ask God to show you:

- What lies am I believing about myself?
- What lies am I believing about You, God?
- Where is God in the picture?
- Whose face am I putting on God?

Then use your spiritual weapons of warfare to break free from the handle you've given the enemy by allowing these lies and emotions to reign on the throne of your life. As God speaks His truth to your heart, you will then experience renewed and even deeper intimacy with Him.

2. *Do I have God's heart toward myself and others, or am I aligning with the enemy's thoughts and words?*

Am I seeing myself as God sees me and seeing others as He sees them? Are my thoughts and words uplifting and hopeful (aligning with God's) or critical and negative (aligning with the enemy's)? It's helpful to pray, "Lord, help me to see what You see and to feel what You feel about _____ (person or circumstance)."

In addition to having God's heart toward yourself and others, it is also important that you have God's heart toward the future, which would include sharing in His passion and plans for the Millennium, Jerusalem, Israel, and the biblical feasts! That is the focus of the next few chapters, so be sure to keep reading!

Chapter 5

What Is God's Next Move?

Do you know what the future holds? What's next in God's plan for you? Knowing the answers to these questions is critical for standing strong and unshaken in uncertain, turbulent times. Proverbs 29:18 tells us that without a vision the people will perish. That was never more true than it is today! Without a vision for the future in these uncertain end times—without a clear picture of who Jesus will be when He returns, what He will be doing, and what we will be doing with Him—we will perish. That is, we will be deceived, fall away, our hearts will fail from fear, we will be unable to face persecution, and we will be ineffective as lights through which God can release His end-times purposes.

Future Focus

As I write each chapter of this book, I continue to be challenged to apply each and every word. With so many horrors surrounding us—terror attacks occurring all over the world, threats of terrorists infiltrating our country with the refugees, our borders not being secure to protect us, the imminent signs of the harlot Babylon religion appearing everywhere, the inevitable persecution that is coming upon the church—it's easy to be fearful, negative, depressed, and even shut down. It seems this increasingly dreadful news is in our face everywhere we turn. I have not felt love, joy, peace, the fruits of the spirit all week. When I asked God why not, He showed me that lately I have been focusing only upon how things will get worse and the challenges that await us *prior* to Jesus' return, but I have failed to focus on what I have to look forward to *after* Jesus returns! I believe this focus is another key anchor that will keep us standing strong as lights for the Lord, exhibiting the fruits of the Spirit, *until* He returns.

We must take our eyes off of what we can see now and focus them on the future that awaits us with Jesus. We need to view the uncertainty, the unrighteousness, the immorality around us as temporary, with our hope and our eyes set on what lies ahead! This will give us hope, certainty, and joy in the midst of an increasingly dark world. Often, the Scriptures tell us to set our *hope* on *His return*:

> *Set your hope on the grace to be brought to you when Jesus Christ is revealed at his coming* (1 Peter 1:13 NIV).

> *But we know that when Christ appears, we shall be like him, for we shall see him as he is. All who have this hope in him purify themselves, just as he is pure* (1 John 3:2-3 NIV).

> *Looking for the blessed hope and glorious appearing of our great God and Savior Jesus Christ* (Titus 2:13).

In my opinion, there is currently not enough emphasis in the church on teaching the specifics about Jesus' return, such as what He will be like, what we will be doing, how this world will look, and how all of our social systems will be functioning—government, politics, agriculture, environment, economics, education, law enforcement, media, arts, and technology.

Too many within the church and in the world are still focusing on a Christmas version of Jesus—the sweet baby Jesus lying in the manger, or the meek and mild shepherd with a lamb wrapped around the back of his neck. This is not the Jesus who is coming back soon, nor the one we need to know in order to stand strong, firm, and unshaken in these uncertain, turbulent times.

Furthermore, as I explained previously, it's impossible to experience intimacy with someone when you only know one aspect of them or when you are not willing to enter into knowing all sides of that person. If you only know one aspect of Jesus—as the baby, as love, or as the meek and mild shepherd—you won't experience the deep intimacy with Him that you'll need to stand strong. The more you know about what Jesus will be like when He comes back—what He intends to do, what His heart and plans are for you—the more you will experience intimacy with Him *now*.

Who Will Jesus Be When He Returns?

First of all, He'll be Jewish! He'll return to a Jewish nation (Israel), a Jewish Temple (Ezekiel's) where Jewish sacrifices will be offered, and He'll be celebrating all the feasts! He will be a mighty warrior who will violently execute *all* the kings of the nations— that's roughly 250 kings! He will fight against all the nations who have come against Jerusalem, and He will strike them with a plague so that their flesh will dissolve as they stand on their feet, their eyes shall dissolve in their sockets, and their tongues will dissolve in their mouths! He will strike every horse with confusion (see Zech. 14:3,12-13; 12:4-9; Rev. 19:21).

He will make war, wear a robe dipped in blood, and strike the nations with a sharp sword! He will tread the winepress of the fierceness and wrath of Almighty God, and blood will come out of that winepress up to the horses' bridles! A sword will proceed from His mouth that kills the kings, captains, mighty men, and their horses from all nations who have come together to battle Jerusalem (see Rev. 14:20, 19:11–19; Zech. 12:3–6).

When you know *this* Jesus:

1. It gives you hope and confidence that evil will not ultimately reign. Jesus will overtake and eradicate all the evil, corruption, terrorism, and governments of the world. He will conquer all, and when you are aligned with this King of Kings you do not need to be shaken by what you see happening now in your circumstances or in the world.

2. It draws you into deeper intimacy with Him because it gives you greater appreciation for what He did for you. That same Jesus who is on the throne as described in Revelation 4, the same Jesus who is a mighty, violent warrior in Revelation 19 and Zechariah 12 and 14, chose to take death upon Himself because He wanted you so badly and He valued you so immensely! That's where your acceptance and worth need to come from, and it has nothing to do with your performance! That warring, conquering King Jesus is married to you *now* and has committed to never leave you. He wants to be with you every minute, He misses you when you are focused on anything else, His heart is ravished for you, He is consumed with you, He can't

stop thinking about you, and He loves 100 percent of you. To me, that is unfathomable! In moments when I truly grasp it, I want to fall on my face before Him! All fear, stress, worries, and burdens fall off of me, and everything comes into perspective. I am able to stand strong in Him and not allow my circumstances, emotions, and other people to control my day. I can be His light no matter how dark the circumstances are around me.

Again, I want to encourage you to declare Revelation 19:11–19 and Zechariah 12 through 14 out loud every day, as well as other end-times scriptures from Daniel, Isaiah, and Ezekiel. Doing this brings me into deeper intimacy with Jesus and lifts my eyes above what I can see now of my own problems and the world's insanity. I can stand strong through His victory. I become excited about His return and it motivates me to do all I can to partner with Him *now* to release His end-times purposes. I know it will do the same for you! Especially in these uncertain, turbulent end times, you need to experience all the intimacy that you possibly can—not with a Jesus who is portrayed only as a sweet baby, but with a Jesus who is a warrior king, making war against all that is evil.

So what will Jesus do *after* He wipes out all the kings of the earth? He will establish His Millennial Kingdom. He will rule and reign over all the earth throughout the Millennium, restoring and implementing righteousness in all the nations, governments, and social systems. We have an amazing future to look forward to, as we will be ruling and reigning with Him in righteousness!

Of the greatness of his government and peace there will be no end. He will reign on David's throne and over his kingdom, establishing and upholding it with justice and righteousness from that time on and forever. The zeal of the Lord Almighty will accomplish this (Isaiah 9:7 NIV).

And has made us to be a kingdom and priests to serve his God and Father—to him be glory and power for ever and ever! Amen (Revelation 1:6 NIV).

You have made them to be a kingdom and priests to serve our God, and they will reign on the earth (Revelation 5:10 NIV).

What Is the Millennium?

It is not possible in just one chapter to provide an exhaustive teaching on everything there is to know about the Millennium, although believe me, I'd love to! Studying and teaching on the Millennium is truly a passion of mine, but it will have to wait for yet another future book! I will, however, attempt to give you the highlights from Scripture, because I want my excitement about the Millennium to be contagious—not only to give you hope for the future and keep you standing strong, but also to mobilize you to make a difference for today. As you'll soon see, the Millennium will reveal what you *can* do now in the midst of this out-of-control, corrupt, and unrighteous world.

First, a brief overview of the Millennium. In the simplest explanation, the Millennium is the 1,000-year period that begins after Jesus stands on the Mount of Olives, annihilates all the kings of the earth who have come to battle against Jerusalem, and all Israel is saved (see Rev. 20:2–7; Zech. 12; 14). At the start of the Millennium, Satan is thrown into the abyss where he stays for the 1,000 years, Jesus builds His Millennial Temple in Jerusalem, and begins His reign as King over all the earth!

Satan Bound

He seized the dragon, that ancient serpent, who is the devil, or Satan, and bound him for a thousand years. He threw him into the Abyss, and locked and sealed it over him, to keep him from deceiving the nations anymore until the thousand years were ended. After that, he must be set free for a short time (Revelation 20:2-3 NIV).

When the thousand years are over, Satan will be released from his prison (Revelation 20:7 NIV).

Millennial Temple Built

Thus says the Lord of hosts, "Behold, a man whose name is Branch, for He will branch out from where He is; and He will build the temple of the Lord" (Zechariah 6:12 NASB).

It is he who will build the temple of the Lord, and he will be clothed with majesty and will sit and rule on his throne. And he will be a priest on his throne. And there will be harmony between the two (Zechariah 6:13 NIV).

Jesus Reigns as King

And the Lord will be king over all the earth; in that day the Lord will be the only one, and His name the only one (Zechariah 14:9 NASB).

What Will You Be Doing in the Millennium?

Have you ever thought about what you will be doing after you die or are raptured up in the clouds with Jesus? Many of us picture it like the ultimate vacation or perhaps the perfect retirement community. We will finally catch up on our rest, lie around on the clouds, and nothing will be expected of us. Now that might sound fun and enticing for a few days or even a few weeks, but I think at some point most of us would get pretty bored! As I heard one teacher put it, "We'll wish we would have brought more magazines to read while we are floating around on the clouds!" Well, I've got good news! As usual, what God has planned for you is exceedingly better than all you could ever think, ask, or imagine! You will actually be ruling and reigning with Jesus! You will be "working," but with the perfect boss, finally implementing righteousness throughout all the nations of the earth!

> *You have made them to be a kingdom and priests to serve our God, and they will reign on the earth* (Revelation 5:10 NIV).

> *Or do you not know that the Lord's people will judge the world? ...Do you not know that we will judge angels? How much more the things of this life!* (1 Corinthians 6:2-3 NIV)

> *And has made us to be a kingdom and priests to serve his God and Father—to him be glory and power for ever and ever!* (Revelation 1:6 NIV)

> *They will be priests of God and of Christ and will reign with him for a thousand years* (Revelation 20:6 NIV).

> *And he said to him, "Well done, good servant; because you were faithful in a very little, have authority over ten cities"* (Luke 19:17).

> *Then the sovereignty, power and greatness of all the kingdoms under heaven will be handed over to the holy*

*people of the Most High. His kingdom will be an everlast-
ing kingdom, and all rulers will worship and obey him*
(Daniel 7:27 NIV).

*But the saints of the Highest One will receive the kingdom
and possess the kingdom forever, for all ages to come*
(Daniel 7:18 NASB).

But wait! There's even more to look forward to.

What Will You Look Like in the Millennium?

You will be ruling and reigning with Jesus implementing righteousness throughout the earth in perfect, spiritual, immortal
bodies. Those who you will be ruling over (the tribulation survivors and their children) will have physical, mortal bodies.

*So will it be with the resurrection of the dead. The body
that is sown is perishable, it is raised imperishable; it is
sown in dishonor, it is raised in glory; it is sown in weakness, it is raised in power; it is sown a natural body, it is
raised a spiritual body...in a flash, in the twinkling of an
eye, at the last trumpet. For the trumpet will sound, the
dead will be raised imperishable, and we will be changed.
For the perishable must clothe itself with the imperishable,
and the mortal with immortality* (1 Corinthians 15:42-
44,52,53 NIV).

*Never again will there be in it an infant who lives but a
few days, or an old man who does not live out his years;
the one who dies at a hundred will be thought a mere
child; the one who fails to reach a hundred will be considered accursed* (Isaiah 65:20 NIV).

A priest must not defile himself by going near a dead person; however, if the dead person was his father or mother, son or daughter, brother or unmarried sister, then he may defile himself (Ezekiel 44:25 NIV).

Where Will You Live in the Millennium?

You'll be living in the New Jerusalem—that perfect place Jesus has been preparing for the past 2,000 years—just for you! I don't know about you, but I can't wait until the Millennium!

And he carried me away in the Spirit to a great and high mountain, and showed me the holy city, Jerusalem, coming down out of heaven from God (Revelation 21:10 NASB).

And I saw the holy city, new Jerusalem, coming down out of heaven from God, made ready as a bride adorned for her husband (Revelation 21:2 NASB).

I will write on him...the name of the city of My God, the new Jerusalem, which comes down out of heaven from My God, and My new name (Revelation 3:12 NASB).

For he was looking for the city which has foundations, whose architect and builder is God.... Therefore God is not ashamed to be called their God; for He has prepared a city for them (Hebrews 11:10,16 NASB).

In My Father's house are many dwelling places; if it were not so, I would have told you; for I go to prepare a place for you. If I go and prepare a place for you, I will come again and receive you to Myself, that where I am, there you may be also (John 14:2-3 NASB).

What Will It Be Like in the Millennium?

My husband is originally from New York City, and before our daughter was born we would go to Times Square for New Year's Eve every year. I loved the crowds, the excitement, and how the streets would completely light up with an all-consuming white brilliance (and confetti) at midnight—there's nothing like it in the world!

Just as the ball dropped and the new year was ushered in, John Lennon's "Imagine" would blast through the air. In my opinion, this song is a New Age anthem and a foreshadowing of the Revelation 17 and 18 harlot Babylon (one-world) religion where there is no heaven, no hell, no religion, no countries, and no possessions—and as a result, the world will live as one. However, for the crowd that night, the song is a symbol of hope for the coming new year. Everyone sings along to "Imagine all the people living life in peace," because that is the longing in everyone's heart. Unfortunately, they don't realize the repercussions that these lyrics have had over the past 40 years in desensitizing us to the one world religion! I'm getting off on a tangent here and I'd better refocus! The point is, we all have this longing in our hearts for a world that is at peace—no more wars, conflicts, hunger, pain, or injustice.

Well, that longing we all have is finally satisfied and fulfilled in the Millennium! Let's take a quick sneak peek at what it will look like and what we have to look forward to in the Millennium.

Our Work

Have you ever worked for a difficult boss? Perhaps they placed unreasonable demands on you, expected you to work miracles with no resources, played favorites in the department, or didn't appreciate your efforts. Perhaps they were unqualified for their position, dishonest, controlling, or manipulative. Well, those days will be over! Can you *imagine* what it will be like to have the perfect boss? One who values you and your inputs, provides all the resources that you need, never puts undue pressure on you, treats everyone fairly, recognizes and appreciates your accomplishments, views you as a partner with Him in establishing righteousness and rebuilding the nations of the earth? That's what you have to look forward to in the Millennium!

Have you ever been in a job or role that just wasn't right for you? I spent nearly 40 years of my life in those types of roles! One of the catalysts that eventually lead me to God was trying to find a job that my heart was into, that I believed in, and that was a natural fit for me. It wasn't until God began to open the door for me to teach in ministry on a full-time basis in my mid-40s that I finally found my perfect job fit! Can you *imagine* always being in a role that is perfectly suited for you? One for which you've had years to prove in smaller roles that you were capable and trustworthy to handle? That's what you have to look forward to in the Millennium!

Our Government

Have you ever complained about the corruption and inefficiencies in our government, how much of our taxpayer dollars are wasted, the blindness and deception among our leaders, the injustices in our judicial system, or our huge national deficit? I'm sure we all have at one time or another! Can you *imagine* a government that functions perfectly, based on the Word of God, where everything is ruled in righteousness by honest and fair judges and government leaders? Where there is justice, morality, no corruption, no debt, and zero waste? That's what you have to look forward to in the Millennium!

Our Environment

Do you ever get discouraged by all of the reports of toxic chemicals in our environment and food? Every day there's new research revealing another food which causes cancer or some other serious disease. We fear getting deadly diseases from pesticides and processed or genetically made foods packed with toxic chemicals and sugar. We wonder will there soon be nothing that is safe to eat? Can you *imagine* an environment where the earth will look like the Garden of Eden? Where there will be no pollution, no toxic chemicals, pesticides, waste products, GMOs, non-organic or processed foods? That's what you have to look forward to in the Millennium!

Our Culture

Do you ever become frustrated and grieved by how secular, ungodly, and over-sexed our culture has become? Christians are mocked in TV and movies. Soon they will be seen as the enemies of world peace, love, and tolerance. Secularism and immorality reign in our education system, universities, and entertainment industries. Churches are empty in many countries, or filled with those who prefer "feel good" messages over the whole truth of God. Can you *imagine* a world where His Word will go forth from Zion and cover the earth as the water covers the seas? Where you will have teaching ministries to those you rule over, and once again His Word will be the ruling document in education and governments, and media and the arts will glorify God? There will be no more pornography, sex trafficking, same-sex marriage, divorce, broken families, false religions, racial wars, or rioting. All the nations, peoples, and animals will live together in harmony (sounds like a '70s Coke commercial). That's what you have to look forward to in the Millennium!

Our Health/Bodies

Do you worry about your health and the risk of cancer, Alzheimer's, diabetes, heart attack, stroke, and more? Can you *imagine* a world where you will have a perfect spiritual body, never again to experience sickness? No aches, pains, aging, or imperfections of any kind? That's what you have to look forward to in the Millennium!

Our Homes

Imagine your dream home. Would it be on the beach, on a ranch, or in the mountains at a ski resort? What Jesus is preparing for you now in the New Jerusalem is truly above all that you could ever think, ask, or imagine. I picture beachfront with trees and mountains all around, similar perhaps to 1920s Southern California, with colors as vivid and exquisite as those found in Alaska. A few years back, I had the incredible opportunity to spend two weeks at a school of ministry up in Anchorage. Alaska is without a doubt the most beautiful place I've ever visited. Turquoise water, a heavenly spectrum of exquisite, brilliant, never-seen-before colors forming double rainbows across the sky. It is truly "out of this world," and to me the closest thing on earth to what is described in the throne room scene of Revelation 4 and 5. As incredible as the scenery and colors are in Alaska, they provide only a tiny glimpse of what it will look like in the New Jerusalem! That's what you have to look forward to in the Millennium!

What Is on God's Heart for the Millennium?

When you know and align with what is on God's heart for the Millennium, it will increase your intimacy with Him, and it will also direct you as to how you can partner with Him to begin building His Millennial Kingdom *now*! You don't have to wait for Jesus' return! Listed below are ten facets of God's heart revealing what He has planned for the Millennium, along with supporting scriptures. In Chapter 7, we'll explore in greater detail what *you* can do to begin making each one of these desires of His heart a reality *now*.

1. Reigning over *All the Earth as King in Truth and Holiness*

And the Lord will be king over all the earth; in that day the Lord will be the only one, and His name the only one (Zechariah 14:9 NASB).

When the Son of Man comes in His glory...then He will sit on the throne of His glory. All the nations will be gathered before Him (Matthew 25:31-32).

In love a throne will be established; in faithfulness a man will sit on it—one from the house of David—one who in judging seeks justice and speeds the cause of righteousness (Isaiah 16:5 NIV).

The kingdom of the world has become the kingdom of our Lord and of his Messiah; and he will reign forever and ever (Revelation 11:15 NIV).

There will be no end to the increase of His government or of peace, on the throne of David and over his kingdom, to establish it and to uphold it with justice and righteousness from then on and forevermore. The zeal of the Lord of hosts will accomplish this (Isaiah 9:7 NASB).

And to Him was given dominion, glory and a kingdom, that all the peoples, nations and men of every language might serve Him. His dominion is an everlasting dominion which will not pass away; and His kingdom is one which will not be destroyed (Daniel 7:14 NASB).

2. Implementing Righteousness in All Governments and Social Systems

And He will judge between the nations, and will render decisions for many peoples; and they will hammer their swords into plowshares and their spears into pruning hooks. Nation will not lift up sword against nation, and never again will they learn war (Isaiah 2:4 NASB).

But with righteousness he will judge the needy, with justice he will give decisions for the poor of the earth. He will strike the earth with the rod of his mouth; with the breath of his lips he will slay the wicked. Righteousness will be his belt and faithfulness the sash around his waist (Isaiah 11:4-5 NIV).

In love a throne will be established; in faithfulness a man will sit on it—one from the house of David—one who in judging seeks justice and speeds the cause of righteousness (Isaiah 16:5 NIV).

Listen to me, my people; hear me, my nation: Instruction will go out from me; my justice will become a light to the nations. My righteousness draws near speedily, my salvation is on the way, and my arm will bring justice to the nations.... But my righteousness will last forever, my salvation through all generations (Isaiah 51:4-5,8 NIV).

Righteousness and justice are the foundation of your throne; love and faithfulness go before you (Psalms 89:14 NIV).

"The days are coming," declares the Lord, "when I will raise up for David a righteous Branch, a King who will reign wisely and do what is just and right in the land" (Jeremiah 23:5 NIV).

3. *Ruling and Reigning with You in Resurrected Bodies*

And has made us to be a kingdom and priests to serve his God and Father—to him be glory and power for ever and ever! (Revelation 1:6 NIV)

You have made them to be a kingdom and priests to serve our God, and they will reign on the earth (Revelation 5:10 NIV).

They will be priests of God and of Christ and will reign with him for a thousand years (Revelation 20:6 NIV).

Or do you not know that the Lord's people will judge the world? ...Do you not know that we will judge angels? How much more the things of this life! (1 Corinthians 6:2-3 NIV)

But the saints of the Highest One will receive the kingdom and possess the kingdom forever, for all ages to come (Daniel 7:18 NASB).

Then the sovereignty, power and greatness of all the kingdoms under heaven will be handed over to the holy people of the Most High. His kingdom will be an everlasting kingdom, and all rulers will worship and obey him (Daniel 7:27 NIV).

So will it be with the resurrection of the dead. The body that is sown is perishable, it is raised imperishable; it is sown in dishonor, it is raised in glory; it is sown in weakness, it is raised in power; it is sown a natural body, it is raised a spiritual body...in a flash, in the twinkling of an eye, at the last trumpet. For the trumpet will sound, the dead will be raised imperishable, and we will be changed.

For the perishable must clothe itself with the imperishable, and the mortal with immortality (1 Corinthians 15:42-44,52-53).

4. *Bringing Healing and Restoration to All the Earth, People, Animals, and Relationships*

And that He may send Jesus, the Christ appointed for you, whom heaven must receive until the period of restoration of all things about which God spoke by the mouth of His holy prophets from ancient time (Acts 3:20-21 NASB).

Return to the stronghold, O prisoners who have the hope; this very day I am declaring that I will restore double to you (Zechariah 9:12 NASB).

In that day the Branch of the Lord will be beautiful and glorious, and the fruit of the earth will be the pride and the adornment of the survivors of Israel. It will come about that he who is left in Zion and remains in Jerusalem will be called holy—everyone who is recorded for life in Jerusalem. When the Lord has washed away the filth of the daughters of Zion and purged the bloodshed of Jerusalem from her midst, by the spirit of judgment and the spirit of burning, then the Lord will create over the whole area of Mount Zion and over her assemblies a cloud by day, even smoke, and the brightness of a flaming fire by night; for over all the glory will be a canopy. There will be a shelter to give shade from the heat by day, and refuge and protection from the storm and the rain (Isaiah 4:2-6 NASB).

And the wolf will dwell with the lamb, and the leopard will lie down with the young goat, and the calf and the young lion and the fatling together; and a little boy will lead them. Also the cow and the bear will graze, their young will lie down together, and the lion will eat straw like the ox. The nursing child will play by the hole of the cobra, and the weaned child will put his hand on the viper's den. They will not hurt or destroy in all My holy mountain, For the earth will be full of the knowledge of the Lord as the waters cover the sea (Isaiah 11:6-9 NASB).

The light of the moon will be as the light of the sun, and the light of the sun will be seven times brighter, like the light of seven days, on the day the Lord binds up the fracture of His people and heals the bruise He has inflicted (Isaiah 30:26 NASB).

Then the eyes of the blind will be opened and the ears of the deaf will be unstopped. Then the lame will leap like a deer, and the tongue of the mute will shout for joy (Isaiah 35:5-6 NASB).

Indeed, the Lord will comfort Zion; He will comfort all her waste places. And her wilderness He will make like Eden, and her desert like the garden of the Lord; joy and gladness will be found in her, thanksgiving and sound of a melody (Isaiah 51:3 NASB).

Instead of your shame you will have a double portion, and instead of humiliation they will shout for joy over their portion. Therefore they will possess a double portion in their land, everlasting joy will be theirs (Isaiah 61:7 NASB).

For behold, I create Jerusalem for rejoicing and her people for gladness. I will also rejoice in Jerusalem and be glad in My people; and there will no longer be heard in her the voice of weeping and the sound of crying. No longer will there be in it an infant who lives but a few days, or an old man who does not live out his days; for the youth will die at the age of one hundred and the one who does not reach the age of one hundred will be thought accursed. They will build houses and inhabit them; they will also plant vine-yards and eat their fruit. They will not build and another inhabit, they will not plant and another eat; for as the lifetime of a tree, so will be the days of My people, and My chosen ones will wear out the work of their hands (Isaiah 65:18-22 NASB).

And in that day the mountains will drip with sweet wine, and the hills will flow with milk, and all the brooks of Judah will flow with water; and a spring will go out from the house of the Lord to water the valley of Shittim (Joel 3:18 NASB).

I will make them and the places around My hill a blessing. And I will cause showers to come down in their season; they will be showers of blessing. Also the tree of the field will yield its fruit and the earth will yield its increase, and they will be secure on their land. Then they will know that I am the Lord, when I have broken the bars of their yoke and have delivered them from the hand of those who enslaved them. They will no longer be a prey to the nations, and the beasts of the earth will not devour them; but they will live securely, and no one will make them afraid. I will establish for them a renowned planting place, and they will not again be victims of famine in the land, and they will not endure the insults of the nations anymore (Ezekiel 34:26-29 NASB).

I will multiply men on you, all the house of Israel, all of it; and the cities will be inhabited and the waste places will be rebuilt (Ezekiel 36:10 NASB).

On the day that I cleanse you from all your iniquities, I will cause the cities to be inhabited, and the waste places will be rebuilt. ...They will say, "This desolate land has become like the garden of Eden; and the waste, desolate and ruined cities are fortified and inhabited" (Ezekiel 36:33,35 NASB).

In that day I will also make a covenant for them with the beasts of the field, the birds of the sky, and the creeping things of the ground. And I will abolish the bow, the sword and war from the land, and will make them lie down in safety (Hosea 2:18 NASB).

5. Restoring Israel Spiritually and Physically

And I will pour on the house of David and on the inhabitants of Jerusalem the Spirit of grace and supplication; then they will look on Me whom they pierced. Yes, they will mourn for Him as one mourns for his only son, and grieve for Him as one grieves for a firstborn (Zechariah 12:10).

On that day a fountain will be opened to the house of David and the inhabitants of Jerusalem, to cleanse them from sin and impurity (Zechariah 13:1 NIV).

I will sprinkle clean water on you, and you will be clean; I will cleanse you from all your impurities and from all your idols (Ezekiel 36:25 NIV).

They will no longer defile themselves with their idols and vile images or with any of their offenses, for I will save them from all their sinful backsliding, and I will cleanse them. They will be my people, and I will be their God (Ezekiel 37:23 NIV).

And in this way all Israel will be saved (Romans 11:26 NIV).

He will set up a banner for the nations, and will assemble the outcasts of Israel, and gather together the dispersed of Judah from the four corners of the earth (Isaiah 11:12).

Indeed He says, "It is too small a thing that You should be My Servant to raise up the tribes of Jacob, and to restore the preserved ones of Israel; I will also give You as a light to the Gentiles, that you should be My salvation to the ends of the earth" (Isaiah 49:6).

The Gentiles shall come to your light, and kings to the brightness of your rising (Isaiah 60:3).

6. *Bringing Together in One All Things that Are in Heaven and Which Are on Earth in Him. Bringing Heaven (the New Jerusalem) to Earth*

That in the dispensation of the fullness of the times He might gather together in one all things in Messiah, both which are in heaven and which are on earth—in Him (Ephesians 1:10).

Your kingdom come. Your will be done on earth as it is in heaven (Matthew 6:10).

He who overcomes, I will make him a pillar in the temple of My God, and he shall go out no more. I will write on him the name of My God and the name of the city of My God, the New Jerusalem, which comes down out of heaven from My God. And I will write on him My new name (Revelation 3:12).

Then I, John, saw the holy city, New Jerusalem, coming down out of heaven from God, prepared as a bride adorned for her husband. And I heard a loud voice from heaven saying, "Behold, the tabernacle of God is with men, and He will dwell with them, and they shall be His people. God Himself will be with them and be their God" (Revelation 21:2-3).

And he carried me away in the Spirit to a great and high mountain, and showed me the great city, the holy Jerusalem, descending out of heaven from God (Revelation 21:10).

For he waited for the city which has foundations, whose builder and maker is God. ...But now they desire a better, that is, a heavenly country. Therefore God is not ashamed to be called their God, for He has prepared a city for them (Hebrews 11:10,16).

7. *Establishing His Name Forever in Jerusalem—The City of Truth, the City of the Great King, and the Throne of the Lord*

At that time Jerusalem shall be called The Throne of the Lord, and all the nations shall be gathered to it, to the name of the Lord, to Jerusalem. No more shall they follow the dictates of their evil hearts (Jeremiah 3:17).

Nor by the earth, for it is His footstool; nor by Jerusalem, for it is the city of the great King (Matthew 5:35).

I will return to Zion, and dwell in the midst of Jerusalem. Jerusalem shall be called the City of Truth, the Mountain of the Lord of hosts, the Holy Mountain (Zechariah 8:3).

He even set a carved image of Asherah that he had made, in the house of which the Lord had said to David and to Solomon his son, "In this house and in Jerusalem, which I have chosen out of all the tribes of Israel, I will put My name forever" (2 Kings 21:7).

Jerusalem, the city where I have chosen for Myself to put My name (1 Kings 11:36 NASB).

And to Him was given dominion, glory and a kingdom, that all the peoples, nations and men of every language might serve Him. His dominion is an everlasting dominion which will not pass away; and His kingdom is one which will not be destroyed (Daniel 7:14 NASB).

8. *Being Worshiped by All People and Nations from Every Tribe and Tongue in the Millennial Temple in Jerusalem*

After these things I looked, and behold, a great multitude which no one could number, of all nations, tribes, peoples, and tongues, standing before the throne and before the Lamb, clothed with white robes, with palm branches in their hands (Revelation 7:9).

Great and marvelous are Your works, Lord God Almighty! Just and true are Your ways, O King of the saints! Who shall not fear You, O Lord, and glorify Your name? For You alone are holy. For all nations shall come and worship before You, for Your judgments have been manifested (Revelation 15:3-4).

"Worthy are You to take the book and to break its seals; for You were slain, and purchased for God with Your blood men from every tribe and tongue and people and nation. You have made them to be a kingdom and priests to our God; and they will reign upon the earth." Then I looked, and I heard the voice of many angels around the throne and the living creatures and the elders; and the number of them was myriads of myriads, and thousands of thousands, saying with a loud voice, "Worthy is the Lamb that was slain to receive power and riches and wisdom and might and honor and glory and blessing." And every created thing which is in heaven and on the earth and under the earth and on the sea, and all things in them, I heard saying, "To Him who sits on the throne, and to the Lamb, be blessing and honor and glory and dominion forever and ever" (Revelation 5:9-13 NASB).

At that time Jerusalem shall be called The Throne of the Lord, and all the nations shall be gathered to it, to the name of the Lord, to Jerusalem. No more shall they follow the dictates of their evil hearts (Jeremiah 3:17).

And He said to me, "Son of man, this is the place of My throne and the place of the soles of My feet, where I will dwell in the midst of the children of Israel forever. No more shall the house of Israel defile My holy name, they nor their kings, by their harlotry or with the carcasses of their kings on their high places (Ezekiel 43:7).

Then speak to him, saying, "Thus says the Lord of hosts, saying: 'Behold, the Man whose name is the Branch! From His place He shall branch out, and He shall build the temple of the Lord; yes, He shall build the temple of the Lord. He shall bear the glory, and shall sit and rule on His throne; so He shall be a priest on His throne, and the counsel of peace shall be between them both'" (Zechariah 6:12-13).

9. Spreading His Word Throughout the Entire Earth as the Waters Cover the Sea

And many peoples will come and say, "Come, let us go up to the mountain of the Lord, to the house of the God of Jacob; that He may teach us concerning His ways and that we may walk in His paths." For the law will go forth from Zion and the word of the Lord from Jerusalem (Isaiah 2:3 NASB).

They will not hurt or destroy in all My holy mountain, for the earth will be full of the knowledge of the Lord as the waters cover the sea (Isaiah 11:9 NASB).

For the earth will be filled with the knowledge of the glory of the Lord, as the waters cover the sea (Habakkuk 2:14 NASB).

Go therefore and make disciples of all the nations, baptizing them in the name of the Father and the Son and the Holy Spirit (Matthew 28:19 NASB).

10. Observing the Biblical Feasts, Festivals, Shabbats, and New Moons

In any dispute, the priests are to serve as judges and decide it according to my ordinances. They are to keep my laws and my decrees for all my appointed festivals, and they are to keep my Sabbaths holy (Ezekiel 44:24 NIV).

In the first month on the fourteenth day you are to observe the Passover, a festival lasting seven days, during which you shall eat bread made without yeast. On that day the prince is to provide a bull as a sin offering for himself and for all the people of the land. Every day during the seven days of the festival he is to provide seven bulls and seven rams without defect as a burnt offering to the Lord, and a male goat for a sin offering. He is to provide as a grain offering an ephah for each bull and an ephah for each ram, along with a hin of olive oil for each ephah. During the seven days of the festival, which begins in the seventh month on the fifteenth day, he is to make the same provision for sin offerings, burnt offerings, grain offerings and oil (Ezekiel 45:21-25 NIV).

The burnt offering the prince brings to the Lord on the Sabbath day is to be six male lambs and a ram, all without defect. The grain offering given with the ram is to be an ephah, and the grain offering with the lambs is to be as much as he pleases, along with a hin of olive oil for each ephah. On the day of the New Moon he is to offer a young bull, six lambs and a ram, all without defect. He is to provide as a grain offering one ephah with the bull, one ephah with the ram, and with the lambs as much as he wants to give, along with a hin of oil for each ephah (Ezekiel 46:4-7 NIV).

And it shall come to pass that everyone who is left of all the nations which came against Jerusalem shall go up from year to year to worship the King, the Lord of hosts, and to keep the Feast of Tabernacles. And it shall be that whichever of the families of the earth do not come up to

Jerusalem to worship the King, the Lord of hosts, on them there will be no rain. If the family of Egypt will not come up and enter in, they shall have no rain; they shall receive the plague with which the Lord strikes the nations who do not come up to keep the Feast of Tabernacles. This shall be the punishment of Egypt and the punishment of all the nations that do not come up to keep the Feast of Tabernacles (Zechariah 14:16-19).

Why Should You Focus on the Millennium *Now*?

1. *Increased Intimacy with God*

It draws you into deeper intimacy with God. When you connect with God's passion and heart for what He has planned in the Millennium—by studying, declaring the scriptures noted above, and partnering with Him to increase His Millennial Kingdom *now*—you grow closer in intimacy with God, which will keep you strong and unshaken in uncertain times!

"What?" you may be thinking. "An end-times teaching that actually draws me into deeper intimacy with Him?" I understand how you feel! Actually, I never thought I would ever be teaching on the end times. In fact, I used to avoid end-times teachings! I always found them to be interesting, but having nothing of relevance that I could apply to my daily life. On the contrary, they would usually end up leaving me confused, in fear, and wanting to hide until Jesus came back!

I was always drawn to teaching that would help me grow closer to God—to experience His love, healing, and freedom in my life—and help me to deal with whatever I was going through! So, the fact that I have such a passion now to teach on the end times is definitely from the Lord and not my own plan! In His great love, He has revealed to me how teaching about the end times and His future plans can be very relevant, practical, and lead to all those things I never thought it could—intimacy with Him, hope, healing, and strength for today!

2. *Excitement for the Future*

It gives you a clear vision of a certain future you can look forward to with much excitement and anticipation—in the midst of these uncertain, turbulent times.

When I become fearful, down, or frustrated with what I see and read in the news—the unrighteousness and corruption; deception among political leaders; shootings; terrorism; antisemitism; poverty; economic debt; natural disasters; immorality blasted through TV, movies, music and Internet; abortion; evil being called good and good evil; when people hurt, reject, disappoint, or frustrate me; when circumstances are difficult and there are job uncertainties, financial worries, fear of not having enough or "making it"—having a clear picture of the Millennium gives me hope and so much to look forward to!

It also removes any expectation that somehow anything or anyone could ever be perfect *now* and helps me to forgive more quickly. As long as there is sin on this earth and Satan is the prince of power of the air (see Eph. 2:2), we can't expect things will ever be perfect. Now don't misunderstand me—that doesn't give us an out or an excuse for doing nothing to fight for righteousness now; actually, quite the opposite! Which leads to me to the third reason you should focus on the Millennium *now*:

3. *A Plan for Action*

Aligning your actions with the facets of God's heart for the Millennium mobilizes you *now* to do what you *can* to make an eternal difference in the midst of a world that feels out of your control and influence.

Never give in to the enemy's lie that this world is too far gone and there's nothing you can do that will make a difference. That's a flat out lie from the pit of hell! Furthermore, it's evident from the Parable of the Talents that it is *never* His will for you to give up or just passively wait around for His return! The wicked, worthless servant in the parable was thrown into outer darkness for this (see Matt. 25:14–30)!

You must never give up fighting for righteousness here on the earth in every social system—government, politics, agriculture, economics, spiritual, education, law enforcement, family, media, arts, technology, athletics, environment—because what you do *now* for righteousness will continue on into the Millennium! When Jesus returns, He will wipe out all evil and anything that stands in the way of love and righteousness. Only that which is made of truth and righteousness *now* will stand forever; therefore the righteousness you establish *now* will "carry over" into the Millennium. You don't have to wait until Jesus returns to start increasing His Millennial reign! That is great motivation to never give up!

Knowing what you can do *now* to increase His Millennial reign gives great purpose, value, meaning, and eternal significance to your daily life! Start each day asking God to enable you to partner with Him to release His end-times purposes!

Even if you don't see the results of your efforts now, you will see them and be rewarded for them in the Millennium. Your role in the Millennium will be determined by your faithfulness in what He's called you to do right *now*!

> *Well done, good servant; because you were faithful in a very little, have authority over ten cities* (Luke 19:17).

Let's explore a few of the facets of God's heart for the Millennium in more detail as they relate to growing in intimacy with Him. First we'll explore His Millennial Temple and then in Chapter 6 His observance of the biblical feasts.

The above is a photo of the Millennial Temple model created by Rabbi Chaim Clorfene and featured in his book, *The Messianic Temple*, Menorah Books, LTD.

The Millennial Temple

We've all heard the old expression, "A picture is worth a thousand words." Visuals stick in our minds and memories much more powerfully than words, and they penetrate the heart in ways that words cannot. Whenever I teach using props and visuals, people always tell me, even years later, that what they remember and what impacted them the most are the visuals! A visual makes a mere conceptual idea real and concrete. That's exactly what I love about the Millennial Temple! It gives us visual, concrete evidence that all of the Millennial promises will be fulfilled.

Our world is changing so rapidly these days! The rate of moral decline, biblical prophecy being fulfilled, and the spread of Islam is happening at a pace that is unprecedented. Not to mention the changes that have occurred due to the rapid rate of continual technological innovations. At this rate of change, I can't imagine what the world will be like even by the time this book is finally released!

Having a concrete visual of the future Millennial Temple, which represents future promises being fulfilled, is an oasis of stability and hope in the midst of all this change. It provides certainty in the midst of all of the uncertainty in our lives and in our world.

Let's review our series of end-times events: After Jesus returns, He defeats all the kings of the earth who have gathered to battle against Jerusalem, all Israel is saved, and He builds the Millennial Temple.

> *Thus says the Lord of hosts, "Behold, a man whose name is Branch, for He will branch out from where He is; and He will build the temple of the Lord"* (Zechariah 6:12 NASB).

> *It is he who will build the temple of the Lord, and he will be clothed with majesty and will sit and rule on his throne. And he will be a priest on his throne. And there will be harmony between the two* (Zechariah 6:13 NIV).

Once again there is a need for another future book in order describe all the details of the Millennial Temple given to us in Ezekiel 40–48, but for now here are a few highlights:

1. *The Millennial Temple is the place of His throne forever— how amazing is that!*

> *He said: "Son of man, this is the place of my throne and the place for the soles of my feet. This is where I will live among the Israelites forever"* (Ezekiel 43:7 NIV).

It is he who will build the temple of the Lord, and he will be clothed with majesty and will sit and rule on his throne. And he will be a priest on his throne (Zechariah 6:13 NIV).

When the Son of Man comes in His glory...then He will sit on the throne of His glory. All the nations will be gathered before Him (Matthew 25:31-32).

In love a throne will be established; in faithfulness a man will sit on it—one from the house of David—one who in judging seeks justice and speeds the cause of righteousness (Isaiah 16:5 NIV).

2. ***God's manifest presence dwells in the Millennial Temple!***

The glory of the Lord entered the temple through the gate facing east. Then the Spirit lifted me up and brought me into the inner court, and the glory of the Lord filled the temple (Ezekiel 43:4 NIV).

I looked and saw the glory of the Lord filling the temple of the Lord, and I fell facedown (Ezekiel 44:4 NIV).

God Is into the Details!

God provides extensive and measurable detail in Ezekiel 40–48 regarding the dimensions of the Millennial Temple and the Temple Mount; the allocation of land to the tribes; the "job descriptions" and dwelling places for the prince, priests, and Levites; when and how the sacrifices will be offered; and specifics about how the feasts and festivals will be observed.

All of this detail reassures us of the certainty of this future temple, the Millennial promises being fulfilled, and how much

God cares about the details. If He cares so much about the details of the Temple, how much more so does He care and desire for you to seek Him regarding every single detail in your life!

Let me digress for a moment to give you a few quick recent examples.

Example #1: "Every last cent"

I have been balancing checkbooks ever since my sister taught me to do hers back when I was in early elementary school. There has never been a month since when I have not been able to get my books to balance down to the last cent. However, earlier this summer there was a month when no matter how hard I tried (and I tried for over five months), I could not get it to balance! I never thought of bringing God into this; why would He be interested? It's just some routine part of life here on earth that I have to deal with every month and that takes time away from doing *His* work. Finally, I decided to pray about it! I thanked Him in advance for shining the light on the issue and revealing the mistake to me. Even though I had been unsuccessful for over five months, within minutes after I prayed God opened my eyes to the error and I was able to balance it perfectly! This experience drew me into deeper intimacy with Him as I was amazed at how much He cares and desires to be a part of every detail of our lives. He wants intimacy with us every minute!

Example #2: "Even the back of an earring!"

A few months ago, I was in my hotel room getting ready to teach at a conference on the Millennial Temple. I was on time, all ready to go, I just needed to put in my earrings. The ones I had brought with me to wear were the diamond earrings that Al gave me for my 40th birthday when I was nine months pregnant with Charis. We were living in Chicago, and our doctor had convinced

Al that it was a "Chicago tradition" to buy your wife diamond earrings when she delivered her first baby. I never argued with him on that instruction! It was a very special time in our marriage, and so these earrings hold a very dear place and meaning in my heart.

As I was leaning over the sink trying to put them in while looking in the mirror, I dropped the backing and couldn't find it anywhere! I searched and searched over and over again; it had to be somewhere! Finally, it was at the point where if I continued to look I would be late for my own teaching. Now, I could have used a backing from other earrings that would fit well enough temporarily, but I just couldn't stand the thought of losing the original one from Chicago. Now remember, this was just the backing I had lost, not the diamond earring itself, so I felt a bit silly praying about it, but I also knew that God knows and understands everything in our hearts. I thanked Him in advance for leading me to it, and within seconds I saw it—right in the same spot where I had been looking for the past half hour! Once again, I felt so loved and drawn into deeper intimacy with Him as I experienced His never-ending love for me in every little detail of my life! So to sum it up and to get us back to the Millennial Temple, God is into the details!

When you connect with the facets of God's heart that reveal what He has planned for the Millennial Temple—by studying the detailed visual plans, declaring Scripture, and looking forward to it with passion and anticipation—it strengthens your faith and intimacy with God, and it provides visual evidence of the fulfillment of these Millennial promises:

1. Jesus will return and reign as King over all the earth.

2. Jesus will implement righteousness in every sphere of life.

3. We will rule and reign with Jesus in our spiritual, resurrected bodies.

4. Jesus will restore and heal everything on the earth.

5. Israel will be restored both physically and spiritually.

6. Jesus will bring heaven to earth in the New Jerusalem.

7. Jesus will establish His name and throne forever in Jerusalem.

8. Jesus will be worshiped by all peoples and nations in the Millennial Temple.

9. We will be teaching His Word throughout all the earth.

10. We will be celebrating the feasts with Jesus.

I can't wait, and I hope you feel the same way too! It's the detailed visual and the certainty of these promises being fulfilled that make the Millennial Temple another powerful anchor for remaining unshaken and standing strong in uncertain times. As promised, in the next chapter we'll explore God's heart for the biblical feasts!

Chapter 6

Why Observe the Feasts?

I love teaching on the biblical feasts for many reasons, but most of all because studying and observing them draws you into such deep intimacy with God. You don't *have* to observe the biblical feasts in that your salvation does not depend upon it, but when you don't, *you* miss out on a blessing and a unique opportunity to know Him more intimately. You see, the biblical feasts are God's special appointments with you. The Hebrew word for feasts, *moedim*, means "appointment." Our God is so amazing that He sets aside certain times of the year to make "personal appointments" with you—times of special blessing, revelation, and intimacy with Him. Now, I'm sure you have an appointment calendar and would never miss hair and nail appointments or important work meetings with your boss or key clients, so why would you ever want to miss a special appointment with God?

When I use the term *biblical feasts*, I'm referring to the "Feasts of the Lord" that are detailed in Leviticus 23:

> *Speak to the children of Israel, and say to them, "The feasts of the Lord, which you shall proclaim to be holy convocations, these are My feasts...these are the feasts of the*

Lord, holy convocations which you shall proclaim at their appointed times" (Leviticus 23:2,4).

Benefits of the Feasts

These are the feasts that God commanded the Israelites to observe for very specific and meaningful reasons back when they were first given—1,400 years before Jesus came to earth. Each feast actually has a two-fold purpose—one as God described in Leviticus (most often tied to agricultural cycles), and a second, even deeper purpose, which is to reveal Jesus as the Messiah.

In the Leviticus 23 scripture above, it's also interesting to note that the word for "convocations" in Hebrew is *miqra*, which means "dress rehearsal or practice." One of the many ways the feasts reveal Jesus as the Messiah is by providing a special preview. Think about going to the movies—you arrive a little early, and you sit and watch the coming attractions. They tell you what is to come, what you have to look forward to in the next season. That is exactly what the biblical feasts do as well. They tell you what is to come, and they give you certainty about what Jesus is going to do when He perfectly fulfills each feast.

In addition, there is so much that you can learn from the feasts about who God is and how He sees you that will bring healing to the strongholds of your heart. And, if somehow all of these benefits aren't enough for you, there are also many other ways to apply what the feasts communicate about end-times revelation, our Jewish roots, and Jewish culture and idioms that provide deeper understanding of the words He spoke in the context of observing the feasts.

Now what do the biblical feasts have to do with remaining unshaken in uncertain times? As I mentioned above, each feast gives you a certain preview of what Jesus has planned for the future. The spring feasts—Passover (or Feast of Unleavened Bread), First Fruits, and Shavuot (or Pentecost)—have already been fulfilled to their complete meaning with Jesus' *first* coming. The fall feasts—Rosh Hashanah, Yom Kippur, and Feast of Tabernacles (or Sukkot)—will be completely fulfilled with Jesus' *second* coming. Let's first explore each of the three spring feasts.

Passover

Jesus fulfilled the Feast of Unleavened Bread (or Passover) at the cross. Just as death passed over the blood on the doorposts of the Israelites' homes during the tenth plague (death of the firstborn) in Egypt, eternal death passed over all who come under Jesus' blood shed on the cross. I wish I could go into detail now about the hundreds of ways that Jesus perfectly fulfilled the Feast of Passover; again, you'll just have to be patient for another future book release. It literally takes your breath away when you see how every single detail of Passover had significance and how perfectly Jesus fulfilled each one. This so powerfully communicates how detailed God is, and it strengthens our intimacy with Him to have this assurance that He cares about every single detail of our lives and has a perfect timing for everything.

> *For I will go through the land of Egypt on that night, and will strike down all the firstborn in the land of Egypt, both man and beast; and against all the gods of Egypt I will execute judgments—I am the Lord* (Exodus 12:12 NASB).

> *When I see the blood, I will pass over you. No destructive plague will touch you* (Exodus 12:13 NIV).

> *The Lord's Passover begins at twilight on the fourteenth day of the first month. On the fifteenth day of that month*

the Lord's feast of Unleavened Bread begins; for seven days you must eat bread made without yeast. On the first day hold a sacred assembly and do no regular work. For seven days present an offering made to the Lord by fire. And on the seventh day hold a sacred assembly and do no regular work (Leviticus 23:5-8 NIV).

The next day John saw Jesus coming toward him, and said, "Behold! The Lamb of God who takes away the sin of the world!" (John 1:29)

Therefore purge out the old leaven, that you may be a new lump, since you truly are unleavened. For indeed Christ, our Passover, was sacrificed for us. Therefore let us keep the feast, not with old leaven, nor with the leaven of malice and wickedness, but with the unleavened bread of sincerity and truth (1 Corinthians 5:7-8).

First Fruits

The Feast of First Fruits was observed three days after the Passover lambs were slain and it celebrated the early barley harvest. The people were commanded to bring the first fruits to the Temple, lift them in the air, and wave them in every direction before the Lord, to acknowledge that all provision and blessing comes from Him and that He is sovereign over all the earth.

Jesus was the first to rise from the dead. He rose on the Feast of First Fruits, and His resurrection was the complete fulfillment of this Feast.

But now Christ is risen from the dead, and has become the firstfruits of those who have fallen asleep. For since by man came death, by Man also came the resurrection of the dead. For as in Adam all die, even so in Christ all shall be made alive. But each one in his own order: Christ the firstfruits, afterward those who are Christ's at His coming (1 Corinthians 15:20-23).

That the Christ would suffer, that He would be the first to rise from the dead, and would proclaim light to the Jewish people and to the Gentiles (Acts 26:23).

Just as the sheaf from the early harvest of barley was a pledge that the rest of the harvest would come, Jesus' resurrection as the fulfillment of the First Fruits is a guarantee that you (the rest of the harvest) will also rise with Him from the dead! You will rise with Him in spiritual bodies and rule and reign with Him throughout the Millennium!

So will it be with the resurrection of the dead. The body that is sown is perishable, it is raised imperishable; it is sown in dishonor, it is raised in glory; it is sown in weakness, it is raised in power; it is sown a natural body, it is raised a spiritual body...in a flash, in the twinkling of an eye, at the last trumpet. For the trumpet will sound, the dead will be raised imperishable, and we will be changed. For the perishable must clothe itself with the imperishable, and the mortal with immortality (1 Corinthians 15:42-44,52-53 NIV).

Remember, Jesus' followers observed the Feast of First Fruits and therefore knew the deep significance of what Jesus' resurrection on that day meant for them. I'm sure it gave them confidence and boldness in the face of persecution, and it should do the same for you. You can be certain of your future with Him. You don't have to fear what is going on in the world around you or be passive. Instead, like Jesus' early followers, you can be confident and boldly take action to partner with Him in building His Kingdom here on earth!

Shavuot

Shavuot, or the Feast of Weeks, first occurred when God's Word (Torah) was given to the Israelites 3,300 years ago on Mount Sinai, seven weeks (or 50 days) after Passover. God commanded the observance of Shavuot in the following passage from Leviticus:

You shall also count for yourselves from the day after the sabbath (first day of Passover), *from the day when you brought in the sheaf of the wave offering* (barley); *there shall be seven complete sabbaths. You shall count fifty days to* (or until) *the day after the seventh sabbath; then you shall present a new grain offering* (wheat) *to the Lord* (Leviticus 23:15-16 NASB).

The Lord said to Moses, "I am going to come to you in a dense cloud, so that the people will hear me speaking with you and will always put their trust in you." Then Moses told the Lord what the people had said. And the Lord said to Moses, "Go to the people and consecrate them today and tomorrow. Have them wash their clothes and be ready by the third day, because on that day the Lord will come down on Mount Sinai in the sight of all the people" (Exodus 19:9-11 NIV).

On the Feast of Shavuot in Temple times, millions would carry baskets full of first fruits of the latter harvest—wheat, figs, grapes, dates, pomegranates, olives, and barley. They would wave them in the temple and lay prostrate in gratitude for His provision.

The Feast of Shavuot was fulfilled when the Holy Spirit came upon the disciples in the book of Acts, 50 days after Passover. Just as the harvest of Shavuot was a guarantee of the fall harvest, the Holy Spirit at Shavuot was a guarantee of the rest of God's promises.

When the day of Pentecost had come, they were all together in one place. And suddenly there came from heaven a noise like a violent rushing wind, and it filled the whole house where they were sitting. And there appeared to them tongues as of fire distributing themselves, and they rested on each one of them. And they were all filled with the Holy Spirit and began to speak with other tongues, as the Spirit was giving them utterance (Acts 2:1-4 NASB).

In Him you also trusted, after you heard the word of truth, the gospel of your salvation; in whom also, having believed, you were sealed with the Holy Spirit of promise, who is the guarantee of our inheritance until the redemption of the purchased possession, to the praise of His glory (Ephesians 1:13-14).

What are the rest of God's promises that Shavuot guarantees us will be "harvested in the fall"?

They are the following Millennial promises which we covered in Chapter 5:

1. Jesus will return and reign as King over all the earth.

2. Jesus will implement righteousness in every sphere of life.

3. We will rule and reign with Jesus in our spiritual, resurrected bodies.

4. Jesus will restore and heal everything on the earth.

5. Israel will be restored both physically and spiritually.

6. Jesus will bring heaven to earth in the New Jerusalem.

7. Jesus will establish His name and throne forever in Jerusalem.

8. Jesus will be worshiped by all peoples and nations in the Millennial Temple.

9. We will be teaching His Word throughout all the earth.

10. We will be celebrating the feasts with Jesus.

When we begin to think more deeply about the fall feasts, it becomes incredibly exciting as we can more clearly see these feasts as anchors for standing strong in uncertain times.

Again, the fall feasts have not yet been fulfilled, but will be with Jesus' second coming. Every year when we celebrate the fall feasts, it builds our faith and intimacy with God as we are reminded that just as Jesus fulfilled each of the spring feasts with perfect detail and timing, we have *certainty* that He will do the same for each of the fall feasts when He returns!

With all of the uncertainty surrounding us, having this degree of certainty in what is going to happen is both exciting and a rock that helps us stand strong and unshaken. It builds our faith and intimacy with God in the midst of a crazy, turbulent world!

Let's now dig in and briefly explore each of the fall feasts!

Rosh Hashanah

The first fall feast is Rosh Hashanah—the biblical commandment to celebrate Rosh Hashanah comes from Leviticus. Rosh Hashanah is most commonly known as the "Day of Trumpet Blasting."

> *In the seventh month on the first day of the month you shall have rest, a reminder* (memorial) *by blowing of trumpets, a holy convocation. You shall not do any laborious work* (Leviticus 23:23-25 NASB).

Rosh Hashanah means "Head of the Year," and it is the first day of the year on Israel's civil or agricultural calendar, which begins with the month of Tishri. The beginning of the religious calendar is Nisan (Passover is the 14th of Nisan). Rosh Hashanah usually falls in the month of September on our calendar.

Repentance is the main theme of Rosh Hashanah, and I believe that the blowing of the shofar is a wakeup call to repent in preparation for Jesus' return.

It's very interesting to note that the Feast of Rosh Hashanah was also referred to as the day of the "last trump." This is because the shofar is sounded each day throughout the preceding month of Elul as a call to repentance. It is a time of introspection and reviewing of one's deeds and spiritual progress over the past year. Therefore, when the shofar was blown on Rosh Hashanah, the first of Tishri, it was known as the *"last trump."*

Where else in Scripture do we read about the last trump? You got it! Jesus' return!

> *In a flash, in the twinkling of an eye, at the last trumpet. For the trumpet will sound, the dead will be raised imperishable, and we will be changed. For the perishable must*

clothe itself with the imperishable, and the mortal with immortality (1 Corinthians 15:52-53 NIV).

For the Lord Himself will descend from heaven with a shout, with the voice of an archangel, and with the trumpet of God. And the dead in Christ will rise first. Then we who are alive and remain shall be caught up together with them in the clouds to meet the Lord in the air. And thus we shall always be with the Lord (1 Thessalonians 4:16-17).

In Revelation, we also see a relationship between the "last trumpet" blown for the final (seventh) trumpet judgment and the return of Jesus as King, reigning over all the earth.

*The **seventh angel sounded his trumpet**, and there were loud voices in heaven, which said: "The kingdom of the world has become the kingdom of our Lord and of his Messiah, and he will reign for ever and ever." And the twenty-four elders, who were seated on their thrones before God, fell on their faces and worshiped God, saying: "We give thanks to you, Lord God Almighty, the One who is and who was, because you have taken your great power and have begun to reign. The nations were angry, and your wrath has come. The time has come for judging the dead, and for rewarding your servants the prophets and your people who revere your name, both great and small— and for destroying those who destroy the earth"* (Revelation 11:15-18).

Lastly, in Matthew, Jesus Himself foretold that He would return with the sound of a loud trumpet call.

Then the sign of the Son of Man will appear in heaven, and then all the tribes of the earth will mourn, and they will see the Son of Man coming on the clouds of heaven with power and great glory. And He will send His angels with a great sound of a trumpet, and they will gather together His elect from the four winds, from one end of heaven to the other (Matthew 24:30-31).

We see from all of these scriptures that there is a clear and direct relationship between the Feast of Rosh Hashanah and the return of Jesus to rule and reign over the earth. This should give you tremendous confidence and excitement to know with certainty that He will perfectly fulfill the Feast of Rosh Hashanah. Every year when you observe it, Rosh Hashanah will be an anchor for your soul in uncertain times because no matter how out of control the world is at that time, you know with certainty that He is coming back to rule and reign in righteousness and that just as He completely fulfilled the spring feasts He will completely fulfill the fall feast of Rosh Hashanah!

Yom Kippur

Let's move on to the next fall feast, that of Yom Kippur! Yom Kippur occurs on the tenth day of Tishri, ten days after Rosh Hashanah. The biblical commandment to observe Yom Kippur is found in Leviticus:

Also the tenth day of this seventh month shall be the Day of Atonement. It shall be a holy convocation for you; you shall afflict your souls, and offer an offering made by fire to the Lord. And you shall do no work on that same day, for it is the Day of Atonement, to make atonement for you before the Lord your God (Leviticus 23:27-28).

Yom Kippur is also referred to as the "Day of Atonement" or covering. Whereas Passover relates to individual atonement,

Yom Kippur is all about national atonement. It provided a covering over the nation of Israel for an entire year so that they could worship God and come into His manifest presence in the Temple (or tabernacle).

On that day, the High Priest was required to make atonement for the Holy of Holies, the Sanctuary, the Altar, himself and his family, and the nation of Israel. It was the only day of the year the High Priest could enter into the Holy of Holies, and he would practice for that one special day all year long! A full week before Yom Kippur, he would leave his home and family and withdraw to his chamber in the Temple—to study, practice, and to be set apart. Everything he did in the Holy of Holies had to be performed with utmost precision, and absolute perfection was required! For example, without using his hands, he had to transfer a certain amount of incense from a vessel directly into both of his palms at the same time—and not even *one* grain of incense could fall! No wonder he practiced for an entire year! Throughout that day, He was required to make five full immersions in a ritual bath. When he exited the Holy of Holies, he would need to change his clothes before coming into contact with anyone. This was protection for the people so they wouldn't burn up from the holiness emitted from clothing worn in the Holy of Holies!

I have personally experienced deep healing of strongholds from these facts about Yom Kippur because they tell me so much about who God is and how He sees me! He is so holy that absolute perfection is required in the Holy of Holies, yet the Book of Hebrews tells me that you and I can enter into the Holy of Holies at any time!

In Jesus, you have access with boldness and confidence (see Eph. 3:12); you can approach God's throne of grace with boldness (see Heb. 4:16); and you have confidence to enter the Most Holy Place by the blood of Jesus (see Heb. 10:19).

What does that say about how He sees you? You are perfect in His eyes. When He looks at you, He doesn't look at your imperfections; He sees you as the finished product He created you to be! The next time you are intimidated perhaps by a new group of people or with others you perceive as better, more important, or more accomplished than you are, picture yourself as God sees you in the Holy of Holies—perfect before Him. I guarantee you'll never be intimidated again when you see yourself as He sees you!

I get so excited about all that we can apply from the feasts; they tell us so much about who God is and how He sees us! When you study and observe the feasts, each one brings healing to your heart and draws you into deeper intimacy with God!

How does Yom Kippur give us certainty in the midst of uncertainty? The initial purpose of Yom Kippur as the yearly atonement for the nation of Israel will be completely fulfilled when Jesus returns to the Mount of Olives and all Israel is saved.

> It shall be in that day that I will seek to destroy all the nations that come against Jerusalem. And I will pour on the house of David and on the inhabitants of Jerusalem a Spirit of grace and supplication; then they will look on Me whom they pierced. Yes, they will mourn for Him as one mourns for his only son, and grieve for Him as one grieves for a firstborn (Zechariah 12:9-10).

> On that day a fountain will be opened to the house of David and the inhabitants of Jerusalem, to cleanse them from sin and impurity (Zechariah 13:1 NIV).

And in this way all Israel will be saved (Romans 11:26 NIV).

Every year when we observe Yom Kippur, we have certainty that all Israel will be saved when Jesus returns. We need this certainty as an anchor in the midst of uncertainty to keep us strong and unshaken. Just as Jesus fulfilled the spring feasts in perfect detail and timing, in the same way He will also fulfill the fall feast of Yom Kippur!

Sukkot (or Feast of Tabernacles)

After Jesus leads Israel in victory over all the kings of the earth (as described in Zechariah 12–14 and Revelation 19), He builds His Millennial Temple (see Ezek. 40–48) and begins His Millennial reign on earth where we rule and reign with Him for 1,000 years!

This leads us to our next fall feast—that of Sukkot or the Feast of Tabernacles! Sukkot is a seven-day feast that starts on the fifteenth day of the month, or five days after Yom Kippur. It is also known as the Feast of Booths, because of the commandment in Leviticus to live in temporary booths, huts, or "sukkahs" for seven days to remember how God provided for and dwelled with the Israelites in the wilderness for forty years. They were protected by God's cloud of glory by day and column of fire by night. He provided for their every need so that in all of those years of wandering through the desert, their clothes did not wear out, not even the sandals on their feet (see Deut. 29:5)!

Say to the Israelites: "On the fifteenth day of the seventh month the Lord's Festival of Tabernacles begins, and it lasts for seven days. The first day is a sacred assembly; do no regular work. For seven days present food offerings to the Lord, and on the eighth day hold a sacred assembly and present a food offering to the Lord. It is the closing special assembly; do no regular work" (Leviticus 23:34-36 NIV).

So beginning with the fifteenth day of the seventh month, after you have gathered the crops of the land, celebrate the festival to the Lord for seven days; the first day is a day of sabbath rest, and the eighth day also is a day of sabbath rest. On the first day you are to take branches from luxuriant trees—from palms, willows and other leafy trees—and rejoice before the Lord your God for seven days. Celebrate this as a festival to the Lord for seven days each year. This is to be a lasting ordinance for the generations to come; celebrate it in the seventh month. Live in temporary shelters for seven days: All native-born Israelites are to live in such shelters so your descendants will know that I had the Israelites live in temporary shelters when I brought them out of Egypt. I am the Lord your God (Leviticus 23:39-43 NIV).

The themes of Sukkot—God's provision, protection, constant enveloping presence dwelling with us—will be perfectly fulfilled in the Millennium when once again He will dwell with us, ruling and reigning over all the earth!

This feast is so important to God's heart that any nation who does not go up to Jerusalem during the Millennium to celebrate the Feast of Tabernacles will have no rain, and Egypt is told they will experience plagues!

And the Lord shall be King over all the earth. In that day it shall be—"The Lord is one," and His name one (Zechariah 14:9).

And it shall come to pass that everyone who is left of all the nations which came against Jerusalem shall go up from year to year to worship the King, the Lord of hosts, and to keep the Feast of Tabernacles. And it shall be that whichever of the families of the earth do not come up to Jerusalem to worship the King, the Lord of hosts, on them there will be no rain. If the family of Egypt will not come up and enter in, they shall have no rain; they shall receive the plague with which the Lord strikes the nations who do not come up to keep the Feast of Tabernacles. This shall be the punishment of Egypt and the punishment of all the nations that do not come up to keep the Feast of Tabernacles (Zechariah 14:16-19).

There are so many relevant ways to apply the themes of the Feast of Sukkot or Tabernacles in our daily lives, especially relating to intimacy with God. For example, the word *tabernacle* itself means "dwelling." God has desired to dwell with us in a very personal, intimate, and unconditional way all throughout time. We see evidence when He walked with Adam and Eve in the garden in Genesis 3:8 and how He dwelled with the Israelites as they wandered through the desert for 40 years. He was always with them, surrounding them, leading them, protecting them, caring for their every daily need no matter how harsh or scary their circumstances may have appeared on the outside.

We continue to see His desire to dwell with us when He gave Moses the instructions for the tabernacle, which made a way for man to draw near to His manifest presence (see Exod. 25:8); when He filled Solomon's temple with His glory (see Exod. 40:34); when He came to earth in the form of the man Jesus to make the way for us to have eternal life with Him; when He dwells in us as believers (see 1 Cor. 6:19 and 3:16); and when He dwells with us in the Millennium (see Zech. 14:4,9). God desires intimacy with you more than you could ever think or imagine, so don't ever let the enemy come in with His lies about God such as:

- He's distant, unpredictable, against you, with the other person, not there to protect you, not there when you need Him, not interested, disappointed in you, mad at you.

- You can't be good enough for Him.

- He wants you to be miserable.

- He's putting pressure on you.

- He wants you to carry these burdens.

- He's "not in the picture."

- He wants you to figure it out.

- He doesn't have time for the details of your life; He's abandoned you.

- He's with everyone else but you, or He's just watching but not involved in the details of your life.

Every year at the Feast of Sukkot (or Tabernacles), allow it to fill you with excitement from the certainty it provides about the Millennium, the fulfillment of all the Millennial promises, and most importantly God's heart to dwell intimately with you now and forever! Just as Jesus fulfilled the spring feasts in perfect detail and with perfect timing, He will fulfill the fall feast of Sukkot as well!

Shabbat

The Feast of Shabbat is not associated with the spring or fall; rather, it is observed all year long, every week of the year, from Friday sundown to Saturday sundown.

Six days shall work be done, but the seventh day is a Sabbath of solemn rest, a holy convocation. You shall do no work on it; it is the Sabbath of the Lord in all your dwellings (Leviticus 23:3).

The "rest" of Shabbat symbolizes and looks forward to the peace of the Millennial reign with Jesus when everything is restored. For example:

Then the eyes of the blind will be opened and the ears of the deaf will be unstopped. Then the lame will leap like a deer, and the tongue of the mute will shout for joy (Isaiah 35:5-6 NASB).

On the day that I cleanse you from all your iniquities, I will cause the cities to be inhabited, and the waste places will be rebuilt. ...They will say, "This desolate land has become like the garden of Eden; and the waste, desolate and ruined cities are fortified and inhabited" (Ezekiel 36:33,35 NASB).

"The wolf and the lamb will graze together, and the lion will eat straw like the ox; and dust will be the serpent's food. They will do no evil or harm in all My holy mountain," says the Lord (Isaiah 65:25 NASB).

Instead of your shame you will have a double portion, and instead of humiliation they will shout for joy over their portion. Therefore they will possess a double portion in their land, everlasting joy will be theirs (Isaiah 61:7 NASB).

Indeed, the Lord will comfort Zion; He will comfort all her waste places. And her wilderness He will make like

Eden, and her desert like the garden of the Lord; joy and gladness will be found in her, thanksgiving and sound of a melody (Isaiah 51:3 NASB).

And in that day the mountains will drip with sweet wine, and the hills will flow with milk, and all the brooks of Judah will flow with water (Joel 3:18 NASB).

Shabbat is a powerful, weekly reminder of God's heart to restore us both now and in the future, the certainty of the Millennium, and the future fulfillment of all the Millennial promises.

Why It's Important to Observe the Feasts *Now*

I strongly encourage you to study and observe the biblical feasts! Don't miss these special appointments with God, these opportunities to grow in intimacy with Him! Allow them to strengthen your faith in Him and your understanding of Scripture—why Jesus said and did what He did at the time of each feast.

Deeper Intimacy

God designed each of the biblical feasts and chose to use them as a way to reveal Jesus as the Messiah. Undoubtedly, He is passionate about the feasts and they are extremely significant to His heart. Therefore, by studying and observing the feasts you are connecting with His heart, and by that fact alone you will grow deeper in intimacy with Him.

Practice for the Future

Another important reason to observe the feasts *now* is that by doing so you are preparing for Jesus' (your bridegroom's) return and practicing for the future! You will be celebrating the feasts, shabbats, and new moons with Him in the Millennium. The more you practice now, the more you will be prepared for who Jesus will be when He returns and for your role in the Millennium joining with Him in celebrating the feasts.

Anchors for the Soul

Finally, let them be anchors for your soul that keep you standing strong and unshaken no matter what is going on in your life or in the world around you. So much is turbulent and seems out of control, yet we know without a shadow of a doubt that just as Jesus perfectly and completely fulfilled each of the spring feasts, He will fulfill each of the fall feasts and Shabbat in that same manner. Rosh Hashanah gives us certainty of His return, Yom Kippur the confidence that all Israel will be saved, and Sukkot (Tabernacles) and Shabbat the assurance of His Millennial Kingdom and the fulfillment of the Millennial promises! That's certainty for your future that will keep you standing strong and unshaken in the midst of an uncertain world!

Chapter 7

Action Plan

God is not only calling you to remain unshaken in these uncertain times, but also to partner with Him to release His power and purposes in these end times. You now have the anchors you need to stand strong:

- Intimacy with God (Chapter 2) including how to grow in intimacy (Chapter 3) and how to break through barriers to intimacy (Chapter 4)

- Connecting with God's heart for the Millennium, Millennial Temple (Chapter 5) and the biblical feasts (Chapter 6)

What, then, can you do in a world that seems so out of control? How can *you* make a difference when the enemy is telling you that things are too far gone? Remember, the enemy is lying to you because there is so much that you *can* do. When you focus on what you *can* do instead of what you *can't* do or control, you will have no problem being occupied until Jesus returns!

"Focus on what you *do* know, not on what you *don't* know!" That is a word God began speaking to me when I first became a believer. Back then, I didn't know where I was supposed to live, how I was going to make it financially, whether I would ever get married, or whether I would ever find a fulfilling job that was right for me. There was really nothing in my life then that *was* settled or certain, and so I was "forced" to focus on what I *did* know about God rather than what I didn't know about my circumstances.

Today, 27 years later, He's speaking those same words to my heart in a powerful way but in a different context. All of the things that were unsettled when I first became a believer have been settled. There are still many uncertainties now in my life (especially since I began writing this book), but where I feel He's most clearly speaking these words to me (and you) *now* is in relation to the uncertainties and turbulence of today's world. There is so much we don't know—will the economy crash, will terrorism strike here, will there be nuclear war, what will happen to our nation, to our churches, to Christians, to Israel, to democracy, to freedom of speech, religion, and right to bear arms—and He's saying to me (and to you)—focus on what you *do* know about God, not on what you *don't* know about your circumstances.

So, what *do* you know about God just from what you've read in this book? First of all, you know that God desires intimacy with you and that intimacy with Him is the number-one anchor you need to stand strong in uncertain times. Everything you do needs to flow out of a place of intimacy or else it will be your own self-efforts rather than partnering with Him for *His* purposes. Second, you know that you need to be committed to growing in intimacy with Him as well as dealing with anything that blocks intimacy. Third, you know that you experience intimacy with God when you connect with the facets of God's heart revealing His passions for the Millennium, the Millennial Temple, and the biblical feasts.

And what else do you know? It's no surprise or mistake to God that you are alive on the earth right now! He has created and called you for a specific purpose to fulfill at this particular point in time. God can do anything He wants, but for some reason He's always chosen to accomplish His purposes on this earth through man. Starting all the way back in the garden, when He gave dominion over the earth to Adam; continuing with His plans being accomplished through all the prophets and kings; and ultimately through His Son Jesus. Of all the ways God could have redeemed us, He chose to do it through a man. To this day, He still chooses to accomplish His purposes through man—through *you*! The question only you can answer is: "Are you ready and willing to be used by Him, to be a light for Him in these uncertain times, or will you shrink back and remain in fear, frustration, passivity, or apathy?

I know I'm repeating myself, but it is critical that you see this! The enemy wants you to believe that things are too far gone and there is nothing you can do to make a difference. As I've emphasized before, his mode of operation is always to bring death, halt progress, stop life, and set things in backward motion instead of forward motion. He wants you to live in fear and just hide out until Jesus returns. Oftentimes, he entices believers into a self-centered and self-righteous attitude that they will be raptured out of all the world's problems—so why should they care what happens to the world; they're not going to be here! This message is so *not* from God! It's a lie straight from the pit of hell to keep you passive and paralyzed in order that Satan's reign of evil is increased throughout the earth.

It is *not* God's will for you to shrink back and do nothing in these uncertain times due to fear, apathy, passivity, or self-centeredness. It's never His will for you to give up on *anything* and do nothing. Again, remember the Parable of the Talents! God punishes those who hide out and hide their talents—the gifts and plans God has purposed just for them. He always wants to take you into forward motion, never backward, never stopping progress. God has not given you a spirit of fear but power, love, and a sound mind (see 2 Tim. 1:7). He will reward you in the Millennium for how faithful you are now in using the gifts and talents that He's given you toward advancing His kingdom and end-times purposes.

Are you ready to explore what you *can* do to make a difference in these uncertain times? I sure hope so! In order to identify what you *can* do now, remember that you need to know and connect with what is on God's heart. You want to be working in partnership with Him, accomplishing *His* plans for this time not your own self-efforts based on your own wisdom. You don't have to wait for Jesus to come back to begin building His Millennial Kingdom! When you know what is on His heart for the Millennium, then you can identify ways to increase His Millennial Kingdom *now* before He returns. It gives you vision and a point of connection with your future, which not only provides hope but also gives you purpose, motivation, and a "cause" that will propel you out of fear, passivity, apathy, and frustration and into action!

In Chapter 5, I introduced these ten facets of God's heart for the Millennium. Let's explore them now in greater detail in light of how they reveal what God is calling you to do *now*.

The Ten Facets of God's Heart for the Millennium-Action Plan

1. *Reigning over all the earth as King in truth and holiness:*

And the Lord will be king over all the earth; in that day the Lord will be the only one, and His name the only one (Zechariah 14:9 NASB).

I love Zechariah 14:9—only one sentence, yet so powerful, it says it all! He—and no one else—will reign over *all* the earth! Every single aspect of life will be governed by Him! I can trust Him to reign fairly, in perfection and excellence. There will be absolutely nothing to fear with Jesus in charge of everything! Get to know the Jesus of Revelation 19! If this is God's heart for the Millennium, it causes me to think, "What can I do *now* to increase His reign on the earth? In what areas of my life am I not allowing Him to have reign? What strongholds, lies about myself and God, and negative emotions such as fear, stress, criticism, pride, resentment, unforgiveness, and shame are giving the enemy reign over my heart instead of Jesus? Am I allowing Jesus to reign over the way I interact with my husband, daughter, people I meet with throughout the day? Am I allowing Jesus (or someone/something else) to reign over and control my moment-by-moment thoughts, emotions, and words? What do I allow my ears to hear and eyes to see?" There is *so* much you can do to increase Jesus' reign on the earth *now*, before you ever leave your house in the morning!

Another important aspect of increasing Jesus' reign on the earth now is choosing to use spiritual weapons of warfare instead of fleshly weapons in your daily life. Remember, fleshly weapons include worry, fear, stress, panic, blaming others, responding out of hurts and offenses, insisting on winning, revenge, control, manipulation, anger, frustration, complaining, criticizing and bashing others, lying, denying the truth, hiding out, and avoiding conflict and/or people. All of these earthly weapons of warfare increase the enemy's reign, whereas spiritual weapons of warfare increase Jesus' reign on the earth. These would include prayer; fasting; blessing others; giving; praising God; thanking Him in advance in accordance with His will; declaring scriptures out loud; taking your thoughts, emotions, and words captive; asking God to show you what lies you are believing about yourself and Him when you respond with negative, destructive emotions or strongholds; seeing the lies as sin and being willing to cut the ropes you have given to the enemy by confessing, forgiving, and canceling Satan's authority. All of these spiritual weapons of warfare will increase Jesus' reign over your heart and on this earth and align you with the purposes and passions of His heart to ultimately reign over all the earth as King of Kings and Lord of Lords.

2. *Implementing righteousness in all governments and social systems:*

> *"The days are coming," declares the Lord, "when I will raise up for David a righteous Branch, a King who will reign wisely and do what is just and right in the land"* (Jeremiah 23:5 NIV).

> *In love a throne will be established; in faithfulness a man will sit on it—one from the house of David—one who in judging seeks justice and speeds the cause of righteousness* (Isaiah 16:5 NIV).

It brings such joyful expectation to my soul when I think about a ruler who will finally do what is *just* and *right* in the land—throughout all the earth! We have seen terrible injustices in the world; evil, self-centered, demon-possessed rulers and dictators; deceived and weak presidents in our own country. It's so comforting and reassuring to know that every sphere of life here on earth will finally be ruled the way that God intended it to be. Furthermore, what hit me in particular about Isaiah 16:5 was that justice and righteousness would go forth in love and faithfulness! Everything that Jesus will do when He implements righteousness will be out of His love and faithfulness. That will be a first! He won't be ruling out of strongholds such as the need for control, position, fame, and power as do most leaders. He already is *the* preeminent one!

This motivates me to keep fighting for righteousness now and not give up because what I do now will make a significant difference—if I don't see it now, I will see it come to fruition in the Millennium. Nothing that you do now to increase righteousness on this earth will be wasted effort. On the contrary, everything you do to increase righteousness and justice will continue on into the Millennium! But once again, this starts before you even leave your house. Start asking God to show you what you can do to increase righteousness and justice in the way that you speak, think, and interact with your family and co-workers. Be aware of opportunities throughout the day where you have a choice of whether or not to "do the right thing." For example, being completely honest in all matters (no little white lies), tipping adequately, returning extra change that was given in error, reporting all of your tax information accurately, being respectful while driving, returning shopping carts in the parking lot, and the list goes on! You'll be amazed at the opportunities you have to "do the right, just thing" all throughout the day, and every time you do, you are increasing His Millennial reign of righteousness *now!* You don't need to run for President to implement righteousness on the earth! Start implementing righteousness within yourself first, and then out in your social and government systems.

When you are increasing righteousness in those systems, it's critical to remember that what you do *now* to fight for righteousness (even if you don't see the results *now*) will continue on into and make a difference in the Millennium. God is calling you to take a stand for righteousness in your local and national governments, schools, media, arts, and entertainment; to fight for righteousness against injustices and immorality; to vote and use the voice He's given you! Remember, God can do anything, but He chooses to work through you! His will doesn't always get done on this earth (if so, there would be no abortions, murders, terrorism, unsaved souls, etc.), but it *can* get done—through you using your voice and taking a stand for righteousness *now*!

3. Ruling and reigning with you in resurrected bodies:

You have made them to be a kingdom and priests to serve our God, and they will reign on the earth (Revelation 5:10 NIV).

The body that is sown is perishable, it is raised imperishable; it is sown in dishonor, it is raised in glory; it is sown in weakness, it is raised in power; it is sown a natural body, it is raised a spiritual body (1 Corinthians 15:42-44 NIV).

I truly can't imagine what it will be like ruling and reigning with Jesus. Most people we know who are leaders are not willing to share their position of power and authority with anyone, yet the Son of God does? What does that say about His character that He desires to share His rulership with us? What does that say about how He sees us? It's absolutely incredible that He values us so much and desires to be with us so much that He is willing to allow us to rule and reign with Him.

It impacts my life now; for example, when others don't value my inputs and expertise I can still stand strong because I know that Jesus values me enough to desire ruling and reigning with me! Talk about a boost in worth and identity! It also convicts me about how I rule and reign over my own thoughts, emotions, words, and attitudes. If I can't manage those effectively, how am I ever going to be entrusted to rule and reign over nations with Jesus? How am I doing in governing my household? My finances? My time? All of these areas are places that we can practice and prepare for our future, proving our trustworthiness to Jesus for our roles in the Millennium. In every minute of our lives, we have an opportunity to increase His reign by how we govern what He's already given us. Add to this the fact that we'll be ruling and reigning in glorious, spiritual bodies—well, that's something we can all be excited about! We'll never have to worry about sickness, pain, and weight gain ever again!

4. Bringing healing and restoration to all the earth, people, animals, and relationships:

> *Then the eyes of the blind will be opened and the ears of the deaf will be unstopped. Then the lame will leap like a deer, and the tongue of the mute will shout for joy* (Isaiah 35:5-6 NASB).

> *Instead of your shame you will have a double portion, and instead of humiliation they will shout for joy over their portion. Therefore they will possess a double portion in their land, everlasting joy will be theirs* (Isaiah 61:7 NASB).

> *And in that day the mountains will drip with sweet wine, and the hills will flow with milk, and all the brooks of Judah will flow with water; and a spring will go out from the house of the Lord to water the valley of Shittim* (Joel 3:18 NASB).

There are so many scriptures that describe the restoration that occurs during the Millennium, but I chose the above three because I felt they communicated how comprehensive the restoration is that

Jesus has planned. It will include restoration and healing of the land, the atmosphere, animals, humans, relationships, emotions—there will not be anything left untouched, unhealed, unrestored!

What a vision for the future and what hope this brings when everything in this world seems so broken—broken lives, hearts, families, races, the incredible damage that has been done to the earth. It also reveals that if this is the desire of Jesus' heart for the Millennium, it is also the desire of His heart now because He never changes! His heart now is to heal hearts that are open to Him! He always desires to heal hearts and relationships, and there is *nothing* too broken that He cannot heal! If He can restore *everything* on this earth in the Millennium, He can restore *every* heart and life *now*. We can give Him *all* of our brokenness and pain; there is nothing too hard for the Lord! It also makes me think about what I can do to foster restoration and healing in my relationships. Every time I forgive, speak words of blessing toward others, or work toward reconciliation—instead of thinking or talking negatively about others, accusing or being critical of them, staying hurt, or separating and wanting to avoid them—I am building His Millennial Kingdom now. When I use my spiritual weapons of warfare to break through strongholds in my own life, or when I lead others through prayer to do the same in their lives, I am sharing in God's heart for reconciliation and healing, which increases His reign on the earth.

5. Restoring Israel spiritually and physically:

And in this way all Israel will be saved (Romans 11:26 NIV).

Indeed He says, "It is too small a thing that You should be My Servant to raise up the tribes of Jacob, and to restore the preserved ones of Israel; I will also give You as a light to the Gentiles, that you should be my salvation to the ends of the earth" (Isaiah 49:6).

He will set up a banner for the nations, and will assemble the outcasts of Israel, and gather together the dispersed of Judah from the four corners of the earth (Isaiah 11:12).

My heart breaks to watch the rapid rise of antisemitism across the nations, the ever increasing number of daily terror attacks on Israelis by Palestinians trained in preschool to murder Jews, and the international pressure to divide Jerusalem and to give up more land. However, I am strengthened in the promise that one day all Israel will be saved and will experience complete spiritual and physical restoration. Israel will once again regain her God-given position of spiritual leadership and her original mandate as a light to the nations. The land of Israel will be fully restored and given back to the tribes as detailed in Ezekiel 47 and 48. All the land that was stolen from her will be returned as her God-given borders are reestablished.

Just the fact that we have so many beautiful scriptures detailing the physical and spiritual restoration of Israel communicates so much to us about God's heart for Israel. We need to stand with Israel and support Israel in every way possible, because when we do we are connecting with this facet of God's heart and we are sharing in His passion for Israel. As a result, we grow in intimacy with Him, and we help bring about His Millennial Kingdom now! There is so much that you can do to support Israel—with your words in daily conversation as well as with offices of government leaders, in social media, through prayers for their leadership, protection, and salvation, with your financial support, and by studying and connecting with the Jewish roots of your faith. All of these are ways of partnering with God to release His end-times purposes for Israel!

6. *Bringing together in one all things that are in heaven and on earth in Him. Bringing heaven (the New Jerusalem) to earth:*

> *That in the dispensation of the fullness of the times He might gather together in one all things in Messiah, both which are in heaven and which are on earth—in Him* (Ephesians 1:10).

> *Your kingdom come. Your will be done on earth as it is in heaven* (Matthew 6:10).

> *Then I, John, saw the holy city, New Jerusalem, coming down out of heaven from God, prepared as a bride adorned for her husband. And I heard a loud voice from heaven saying, "Behold, the tabernacle of God is with men, and He will dwell with them, and they shall be His people. God Himself will be with them and be their God"* (Revelation 21:2-3).

God's ultimate plan is to bring heaven (possibly the "New Jerusalem") to earth. This fills me with excitement and expectation, especially when I consider that one day God the Father and Jesus the Son will both be on the earth! We have an incredible and a very tangible future to look forward to! The more we do *now* that is in accordance with *His will*, the more we are speeding the day for making this future plan a reality! This assumes, however, that we are in His Word and in prayer *every* day so that we know *His will*. Studying His Word, declaring it out loud, and allowing His Word to guide our thoughts, emotions, words, attitudes, and actions are all ways that we can join with God in His ultimate plan to bring heaven to earth.

Another way that we can align with God's heart to bring heaven to earth is to focus on "the behavior of heaven." By this, I mean knowing what is happening right now in heaven so that you can join in here on earth.

For example, Revelation 5:8-9 tells us that the "behavior of heaven" is characterized by worship—praising God and proclaiming His will or truth through: music (harp), prayer (bowls of incense), and song (they sang a new song). This is the way in which the will of God in heaven is released now on earth, and how the governments of the nations will operate under Jesus' Millennial reign. Revelation 4:10-11 also shows us that that these "behaviors" are demonstrated now by the highest ranking leaders (the 24 elders) as they govern in heaven. Additionally, Hebrews 7:25 and Romans 8:34 reveal that Jesus continually intercedes for us now in heaven.

Therefore, whenever you worship God in music, prayer, and/or song— praising and proclaiming in agreement with His will or truth—you are aligning with God's heart to bring heaven to earth, you are practicing for your future role as a kingdom of priests with Jesus in the Millennium, and you will have a steadfast purpose in the midst of all of the uncertainty around you!

7. *Establishing His name forever in Jerusalem—the City of Truth, the City of the Great King, and the Throne of the Lord:*

Jerusalem shall be called the City of Truth, the Mountain of the Lord of hosts, the Holy Mountain (Zechariah 8:3).

Jerusalem, which I have chosen from all the tribes of Israel, I will put my name forever (2 Kings 21:7).

Jerusalem, the city where I have chosen for Myself, to put My name (1 Kings 11:36).

Jerusalem, for it is the city of the great King (Matthew 5:35).

At that time Jerusalem shall be called The Throne of the Lord (Jeremiah 3:17).

It amazes me to think that of all of the immense universes God created, He chose Jerusalem as the place where He will put His name forever and where He will establish His Throne on the earth. Jerusalem is one special place! No wonder there is such intense spiritual warfare over this small piece of land! Satan is out to kill, steal, and destroy anything that is special to God's heart, and His heart is so tender for Jerusalem. Other verses describe His passion as "fire in Zion" and a "furnace in Jerusalem" (see Isa. 31:9). Zechariah 8:2 tells us that He is exceedingly jealous for Jerusalem. Once again, the more we pray for the peace and protection of Jerusalem, for the salvation of her people, for the city to remain undivided; and the more we use our voices to express support for her; the more we will grow in God's passion for her, grow in intimacy with Him, and help to bring about His Millennial Kingdom now!

8. *Being worshiped by all people and nations from every tribe and tongue in the Millennial Temple in Jerusalem:*

> *After these things I looked, and behold, a great multitude which no one could number, of all nations, tribes, peoples, and tongues, standing before the throne and before the Lamb, clothed with white robes, with palm branches in their hands* (Revelation 7:9).

All nations will come and worship before you, for your righteous acts have been revealed (Revelation 15:4 NIV).

At that time Jerusalem shall be called The Throne of the Lord, and all the nations shall be gathered to it, to the name of the Lord, to Jerusalem (Jeremiah 3:17).

I absolutely love the powerful, beautiful visual that these scriptures describe. Every tribe, tongue, people, and nation will one day worship the Lord together! What an incredible picture of God's heart toward the nations and how He values each tribe, tongue, people, and nation equally in His sight. This convicts me of any prejudice that might exist in my heart, indifference toward the struggles of other nations, fleshly pride in my own nation that would cause insensitivity to the needs of others, as well as any judgment or criticism toward churches of other races or nations. When we pray for unity among races and nations—both inside and outside the body—when we love and pray for other churches and denominations; when we pray for and step out of our comfort zones to extend Jesus' love to people from other races, religions, and countries; when we are quick to take captive any thoughts, emotions, or words that would not be in line with how God sees people from all nations; when we study, pray, and declare the throne room scene in Revelation 4—in all of those ways we are connecting with God's heart, growing in His image and in intimacy with Him, and we are establishing the foundations for His Millennial Kingdom on earth!

9. *Spreading His Word throughout the entire earth as the waters cover the sea:*

And many peoples will come and say, "Come, let us go up to the mountain of the Lord, to the house of the God of Jacob; that He may teach us concerning His ways and that we may walk in His paths." For the law will go forth from Zion and the word of the Lord from Jerusalem" (Isaiah 2:3 NASB).

For the earth will be filled with the knowledge of the glory of the Lord, as the waters cover the sea (Habakkuk 2:14 NASB).

As I mentioned in Chapter 5, finally God's Word will once again be the governing document for all government, education, and judicial systems. It will go forth from Jerusalem as the waters cover the sea! That visual of His Word covering the whole earth is a healing balm to my heart! God's Word will permeate *every* aspect of life on earth! Every time we share truth from His Word—whenever we share our testimony with others, when we support evangelical ministries, mission organizations, and Bible translators—we are connecting with God's heart to spread His Word! And, every time we share or teach His Word (which includes warning others about the upcoming deception, anti-Christ, and one-world religion), we are practicing for our future teaching ministries in the Millennium! Jesus will "employ" us to spread His Word across the entire earth, and I firmly believe this will be a critical element of the entire restoration and renovation process!

10. *Observing the biblical feasts, festivals, shabbats, and new moons:*

In any dispute, the priests are to serve as judges and decide it according to my ordinances. They are to keep my laws and my decrees for all my appointed festivals, and they are to keep my Sabbaths holy (Ezekiel 44:24 NIV).

And it shall come to pass that everyone who is left of all the nations which came against Jerusalem shall go up from year to year to worship the King, the Lord of hosts, and to keep the Feast of Tabernacles. And it shall be that which-ever of the families of the earth do not come up to Jerusalem to worship the King, the Lord of hosts, on them there will be no rain. If the family of Egypt will not come up and enter in, they shall have no rain; they shall receive the plague with which the Lord strikes the nations who do not come up to keep the Feast of Tabernacles. This shall be the punishment of Egypt and the punishment of all the nations that do not come up to keep the Feast of Tabernacles (Zechariah 14:16-19).

God has a special place in His heart for the feasts. They are not holidays that the Jewish people thought up; God Himself designed them—they are *His* feasts! In fact, He is so passionate about them that Zechariah 14 tells us whoever does not observe the Feast of Tabernacles in the Millennium will have no rain, and Egypt will have plagues as well! This communicates to us that we should take His feasts seriously! When we observe and celebrate His feasts *now*, we are aligning with this facet of His heart and thereby growing in intimacy with Him, and we are also practicing and preparing for the future with our bridegroom! We don't want to just show up at these feasts in the Millennium not knowing what's going on or what to do! We want to be prepared so that we can enter into all of the fullness of celebrating with Jesus! In addition to all of the benefits and blessings of partaking in the feasts that were already described in Chapter 6, when we study and observe the feasts we are actually taking part in building His Millennial Kingdom on earth!

IN CLOSING...

If these ten facets of God's heart and what they reveal about God's action plan for you seem like a lot to take in all at once, then just focus on one facet at a time or even one a month! That gives you almost a year's worth of action steps you *can* take *now* to partner with God to release His power and purposes in these end times and to increase His Millennial Kingdom *now*! I can't emphasize this point enough—please don't let the enemy rip you off from God's good and perfect plan for you by deceiving you into believing that things are too far gone, there's nothing you can do that will make a difference, or that you're just supposed to sit and wait or hide out until Jesus returns!

Remember, you have been chosen for such a time as this! Consider it a privilege and an honor to be alive and used by God in these end times. I pray that you will take hold of the anchors detailed in this book—focusing on just *one thing*, intimacy with God, actively pursuing it (offensive moves), being aware of and willing to deal with all barriers to intimacy (defensive moves), and connecting with the facets of God's heart which reveal His passions for the Millennium, the Millennial Temple, and the biblical feasts. In doing so, may you walk on the water with Jesus and experience His abundant life, standing strong and unshaken—not just surviving, but thriving with Him in these uncertain times!

> *Well done...because you have been faithful in a very little thing, you are to be in authority over ten cities!* (Luke 19:17 NASB)

JEANNE NIGRO
MINISTRIES

Jeanne Nigro is a seasoned author/teacher, speaking at churches, congregations, conferences and retreats around the world, and through her television and radio broadcasting platform FACETS OF THE STONE.

Her messages are relevant, practical and life-transforming for both men and women, whether she is uncovering the many facets of God's heart by bringing Old Testament truths to life, healing strongholds of the heart, or preparing believers for Jesus' return.

Real and transparent in the way she shares biblical truth, Jeanne's passion is impacting her audiences to experience greater intimacy with God mobilizing them out of fear, apathy and frustration and into action, as powerfully communicated in her book, "UNSHAKEN: Standing Strong in Uncertain Times."

website: JEANNENIGRO.COM
email: INFO@JEANNENIGRO.COM
FACEBOOK.COM/JEANNENIGROMINISTRIES
TWITTER.COM/JEANNENIGRO

FACETS OF THE ST◆NE

FEATURING AUTHOR/TEACHER JEANNE NIGRO   HOSTED BY DR. KEVIN MCAFEE

Jeanne Nigro's television and radio broadcasting platform FACETS OF THE STONE connects you with the many facets of God's heart. She brings a unique blend of both corporate and ministry experience into her teachings with an MBA as well as expertise in the Jewish roots of our faith. Jeanne's messages are relevant, practical and life-transforming for both men and women, through her transparent and real approach.

Dr. Kevin McAfee is an award winning film producer and director, whose advisory and ministry services in both the faith based and corporate worlds have led numerous top companies, trade associations and political organizations over the past forty years.

Join Jeanne as she uncovers the many facets of God's heart in this unique format which is fun, entertaining, and inspirational, giving you strength for today in these uncertain times!

jn
JEANNE NIGRO
MINISTRIES

website: JEANNENIGRO.COM
FACEBOOK.COM/JEANNENIGROMINISTRIES

email: INFO@JEANNENIGRO.COM
TWITTER.COM/JEANNENIGRO

JEANNE NIGRO MINISTRIES

You won't want to miss these life-changing CD Series:

The Biblical Feasts Collection - It's time to uncover the powerful themes from each feast that draw you into a closer relationship with Jesus, enable you to experience more of His abundant life and freedom, provide an anchor in uncertain times, and prepare you for His return. You'll actually be practicing for the future by applying these amazing teachings!

Breaking Free into God's Presence - Experience victory in the spiritual battle using practical weapons of warfare to break through strongholds such as fear/stress, rejection, anger, unforgiveness, self-condemnation, performance, and more. Get ready to walk in the freedom that is already yours in Him!

What's Next? - Explore how the Millennium and the Millennial Temple give you hope for the future, strength for today, and clear direction for how you can make a difference now in your every day life! An exciting and very certain future awaits you with God!

The Temple Series - What the Temple and its practices reveal about who God is and how He sees you will free you to experience more of His love, healing and power in your life. Delving into these incredible revelations will also help prepare you for Jesus' return!
   - Healing in the Holy of Holies
   - The Millennial Temple

Growing in Intimacy with God - Discover for yourself how intimacy with God is the key anchor you need to stay strong in uncertain times and be a light in the darkness. He desires a whole new level of relationship with you that can be yours as you apply these powerful insights!

Unafraid in these Times - These are turbulent, ever-changing times, but don't let the enemy keep you paralyzed in fear or frustration! Learn how to move into action and fulfill your purpose. You'll see what an exciting privilege it is to partner with God in His plans and purposes for such a time as this!

For more details and order information:
website: **JEANNENIGRO.COM**
email: **INFO@JEANNENIGRO.COM**